TRUE TO YOU:
A REVOLUTIONARY WAY TO GROW YOUR PROFESSIONAL PRACTICE

Rita Johansen

True to You:
A Revolutionary Way to Grow Your Professional Practice
Copyright © 2014 Rita Johansen

Johansen Justice,
P.O. Box 14
Anoka, MN 55303, USA.
www.JohansenJustice.com

Please send permission requests by mail to the address listed above or by email to Johansen@JohansenJustice.com. Thank you.

Publisher and author do not assume responsibility for third-party websites or their content.

Names and identifying characteristics of individuals have been changed to protect their privacy.

The True to You Approach™, The CASA Ask™, Tenacity Ledger Technique™, and The Satisfied-Client Roadmap™ are the intellectual property of Author.

ISBN-13: 978-0-990-7048-1-2

LCCN: 2014917722

DEDICATION

To all dreamers who dare to do.

CONTENTS

INTRODUCTION

When I was launching my solo practice in criminal defense, I had no guidebook to follow on how to grow a business in a profession in which (initially) I was a misfit, and in a practice area in which I was a mold-breaker. You are reading the book I wish I'd had before building my seaworthy vessel and preparing to set sail. In it, I answer the questions I asked often, to whoever was receptive:

- What do you wish you'd known before you launched your practice?
- How do you attract your right-fit clients?
- How do you overcome challenges?
- How do you make networking natural?
- How do you find what you need to grow your business?

During my first year in solo practice, I handled serious felonies, and obtained outcomes for my clients that traditional criminal defenders thought were impossible. As my firm flourished, I prepared to take on an associate to satisfy the **high demand for emotionally intelligent, client- centered representation** in criminal defense—and then medical issues struck and required me to quit. After analyzing what worked to give me success right out of law school, I offer you a way to grow your business that is rooted in practice: the True to You Approach, presented in five parts that work together synergistically.

Part I delves into the inner life of an entrepreneur. I'll show you how to ready yourself to set sail. You'll learn how to cultivate the attitude and willingness needed to **claim your rightful place** at the helm of your customized professional practice.

Part II addresses what to do as you launch: how to build your brand around who you are, and how to find your niche—even when you're a misfit in an un-friendly environment.

Part III dashes the myth that papering networking events with your business card is the best approach to get clients that are the right fit for your firm into the pipeline to your practice. I reveal the **top networking mistake** made by practice owners, and how to make networking natural. You'll also learn how to create a **community of champions** who care about you and (as an extension) help you to grow your business.

In Part IV, I show you how to **attract your right-fit clients**; and share my **misfit-client story**. You'll discover some important **client-relations guide-posts** to follow to transition potential clients into cur-rent clients, and then satisfied former clients.

The last section, Part V, illustrates the dangers of staying at the helm of your ship at all costs. I share **my greatest life lesson**.

Any time is good to apply the True to You Ap-proach, but here's the best one: early on, when your business exists only in the ethers of your imagination.

It's the vision that you yearn to bring to life. Start to build your community of champions around your fledgling business dream. You cannot have too many investors in your success, too soon.

And yet it is never too late to use the True to You Approach to transform your business. Maybe you've taken on clients, but your right-fit clients are scarce. Or maybe things are booming, but you have a nagging feeling that makes you connect with this book. In some way, your business isn't true to who you are.

Wherever you are in the process, I ask that you please have an open mind on our business journey together and a willingness to rethink yourself and your business. What are you waiting for to live out your dreams? Someday is today. You have everything you need within you to build a business that is True to You—and serves your right-fit clients. Go!

AUTHOR'S NOTE

Names and identifying details have been changed to protect privacy. The purpose of this book is to inspire you to prosper in a sometimes unfriendly environment, not to spotlight individuals.

PART I:
UNLEASH YOUR
INNER ENTREPRENEUR

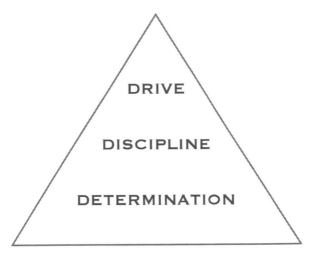

DRIVE

DISCIPLINE

DETERMINATION

THE 3D ENTREPRENEUR

1DRIVE

Entrepreneurs are born, and if you are reading this book, you might be one too. Entrepreneurs become restless when straitjacketed as employees. Hardworking and creative, we make excellent employees, and yet we yearn to be at the captain's wheel. The name for this yearning to create a business enterprise is Drive. It's the first attribute of the 3D Entrepreneur, and it's worthless without the next two: Discipline and Determination. But without drive, discipline and determination will result in a soulless endeavor. (We'll get to those other two in a minute.)

A developing entrepreneur's drive is what makes her eyes light up when conveying in words what exists only in her entrepreneurial imagination. It's the yearning to take that vision and manifest it in this shared reality. And this is why I say that entrepreneurs are born: Drive cannot be manufactured or faked. It comes from within.

Be honest with yourself. Give yourself the freedom to explore your entrepreneurial spirit if you have it, or recognize that you do not have it. I am not creating a hierarchy—contributing as either an entrepreneur or employee has value. A lot of people find great satisfaction in a salaried position. For a time, I was one of them. Everyone is called to create. For some, that calling takes the form of a business enterprise. For me, when this call rose up from within, it was a powerful force.

I learned the hard way to not stifle my entrepreneurial spirit. For eighteen years, I traveled down the employee path. My first gig was counting bracelets into bundles for my uncle's wholesale company. Uncle Andy imported products from foreign lands. Born and raised in tiny Mauston, Wisconsin, I was fascinated as I watched products manufactured "overseas" finding pride of place on an American wrist. I glimpsed a whole new world, operated by supply and demand. Before having formal business training, I learned how a small business worked from the ground up. As Andy's business expanded, my role evolved. I handled client relations and did sales on the wholesale circuit. And then I became his office manager.

I internalized my experiences and lessons, resigned from this business, and went to law school. While there, I did trial team and worked as a student prosecutor in the Community Prosecution Division of the Hennepin County Attorney's Office. The work itself engaged me, and I was creative in my capacity as an employee. Yet I felt stifled. I yearned to take the captain's wheel.

Having enjoyed my work as a student prosecutor, I

figured that the Attorney's Office would be a good place to pay my dues until it was the right time for me to launch my own law practice. I lied to myself, trying to convince myself that criminal prosecutor, any-where at all, was my dream job. I was ready to settle for Someday.

As my clerkship drew to a close, the Office started interviews for two attorney positions. I applied. Busy juggling work projects, school, and trial team, I hadn't investigated my interviewers or even the exact job openings. Determined to make the best of it, I smiled and walked into my interview.

Returning my smile, a sharp-looking, dark-haired male in his forties rose and shook my hand. "How are you doing, Ms. Berg?" he asked. (Berg is my maiden name.)

The short-haired brunette to his left offered me her hand, but not a smile. *They're doing the good-cop, bad-cop routine,* I thought, confident I could crack her.

Without losing my beaming face, I replied, "Fan-tastic! It's not every day you get to interview for your dream job."

My grand entrance was the highlight of the inter-view. I'd ignored the signs—*Civil Attorney! Brake!* — and drove right off the cliff. They inquired about my economics background and my experience in civil law. I spoke about my passion for prosecution, and the classes I'd elected and aced (all in criminal law).

I didn't get the gig, or even a second interview.

Having had tunnel vision centered on the Attorney's Office, their rejection meant I graduated from law school with no real job prospects. I then focused on the brutal licensing test. After successfully filling in the last dot and walking away, I was free to do anything. Later on, I would use this freedom to create a wonderful opportunity. But at first, I floundered.

The post-graduation flurry had ended. I'd defined myself by how many activities I balanced and hats I wore. Hatless, stationary, vulnerable—I had no armor against other people. Their questions jabbed at me.

What do you do? They ask this question as an icebreaker, and sometimes as a filter to decide how much longer to stay in the conversation. They judge your response by the loftiness of the title, the prestige of the field. At the same time, many talked about quitting their jobs to pursue their dreams. Freed, they'd do any number of things. When the individual does not have the time or opportunity to pursue them, these yearned-for activities are as clear to them as a Bora Bora lagoon: start a business, travel, spend quality time with family and friends, or revive a hobby. I never fathomed the shame I'd experience while sharing such a list in lieu of an actual career, many decades before the socially acceptable time—retirement. I felt desperate. *What do I want to do? Who do I want to become?*

It was a taste of the pushback I'd experience as an entrepreneur. After all, who did I think I was? Young.

Female. Unproven. I fantasized about what I would do to defend myself. I'd learn to look the asker in the eye and reply, "I'm Rita Johansen." And I'd be ready for the follow-up question: "What does that mean?" It never came, but if it had, I'd have given this answer: "You don't know what Rita Johansen is capable of. I'm still finding out." And then I imagined the perplexed looks I'd leave in my wake, because those who ask about authority and limitations often lack the capacity to "get it," to understand the entrepreneur's inner life. The desire and potential to create a business mystifies those who do not have it. And even then, I knew that was okay.

For a time, I was not yet ready to embrace my true self. I was still working for somebody else— and stifling my entrepreneurial spirit. And I spent three more weeks living the lie. Lies are dark- colored and sticky. Each one covers our inner barometer for truth with another layer. The thicker the tar gets, the harder it becomes to scrape down to see the truth.

But my truth started to emerge. I didn't care about the prestige of a biography plastered on a large downtown firm's website, or the privilege of shadowing experienced attorneys for three years while doing the grunt work and nothing fulfilling (for me, direct client work). I balked at working in an elite office tower that sealed its windows for fear the depression running rampant through its halls would compel its lawyers to hurl themselves into the street.

Stuffed into the employee box, I had often shown up before the sun rose, or left last, waving forlornly to the security guard before crossing the skyway into the desolate parking ramp. My efforts were fruitless. The Office wasn't hiring a criminal prosecutor, and so out the door I went. I had relied on a political office overgrown with red tape to generate an opportunity for me.

Those layers of confusion and pain (composed of the fear of rejection, the feeling of betrayal for my hard work going unrewarded, the pushback) began to yield to deep introspection, and I reached their root: my opportunities for my life didn't depend upon any-one else.

And this is how *Drive* sets the entrepreneur apart from the employee: drive is the willingness to create the opportunity that allows the entrepreneur to move toward manifesting her business vision. In contrast, an employee has a vision, but settles for a nice-to-have mentality, waiting for somebody else to create the opportunity to achieve this vision. And the em-ployee's vision itself resides within the constructs of someone else's business enterprise. It appears as a po-sition, or a salary goal. For the entrepreneur, the vi-sion relates to the enterprise itself. It's the willingness to create what does not yet exist in this shared reality.

Resolved, I shredded the stack of application ma-terials that I had assembled for attorney positions. I was recovering from the shock of being between jobs in what people (and the news) kept telling me was a brutal economy. "Be grateful for any job," they said. I said, *NO!* I revived the dream I'd tucked away for when I was older, more accomplished, rich, powerful, successful—the bulletproof Someday. Looming large, the entrepreneurial part of me screamed in a way that would be deafening if voiced: *WHY NOT NOW?*

Ultimately, I had to decide whether to masquerade a while longer as an employee, or to unleash my inner entrepreneur based on the answers to these questions: What claim did I want to make about how I operate in the world? Which choice allowed me to contribute in a meaningful way to society, and stay true to my self?

STAKE
YOUR
CLAIM:

ENTREPRENEUR
OR
EMPLOYEE?

I wanted to announce to the world that I was an entrepreneur. I'd dare to manifest in this shared reality what existed in my imagination as my business vision. I gave myself the metaphorical green light—the *go* signal to unleash my entrepreneurial spirit, and it filled me with exhilaration and enthusiasm. And so it began.

Many have this call to create their own enterprises. They have a business vision. Somewhere along the way, they received these messages: Entrepreneurs have an internal compass with true north on it, and an inner roadmap with the path to bring their business vision to life fully charted. They are fearless. And then they wait for the bulletproof vest to form.

This is an inaccurate depiction of the inner life of an entrepreneur, of the emotions behind audacious endeavors. No one is courageous, or afraid, all the time. Courage and fear alternate— sometimes in split-second increments. When courage gets low, fear rises up—and it might seize you by the throat. Then you'll dig deep for why you decided it was worthwhile to leap into the fray. When you grasp the reasons, they resonate with your core and make you radiant. They blast aside fear, and cause courage to rise.

It is true that an entrepreneur has instincts, but the surefire way to success does not necessarily magically appear. She builds her path as she goes. My journey down my business pathway to success has been difficult in places. It's been, at times, terrifying. And I have never had as much joy in my work life. My true joy first started when I decided to pursue my entrepreneurial endeavors.

If you have within you this call to build your own business, then do not hesitate to take the first step to unleash your inner entrepreneur: decide to set sail. I have never heard an entrepreneur regret going for it. But many have stifled their inner entrepreneurs and spent their careers as employees. And this question haunts them: What if?

2 DISCIPLINE

After you unleash your drive, take the time to build a seaworthy vessel. Don't hastily cobble together any old ship, or you set yourself up to sink. Familiarize yourself with the seascape and other sailors —your competitors and the environment. Examine their vessels. What makes them strong?

After I decided to launch my criminal-defense firm, I embraced my instincts and paid attention to my inner voice. An event listing for the Minnesota Women Lawyers' Annual Committee Fair appealed to me, and so I showed up. Instead of sitting alone when I didn't see a familiar face, I sat among the happiest-looking lawyers in the room. I'd unwittingly seated myself at the apex of the Solo and Small Firm Section: solo-practice attorneys flanked me; and across from me sat the section chair. Unaware of the true nature of this happy group, I admitted my decision confession-style, for fear they'd stomp on my budding dream with the boot of skepticism. Instead, they fertilized it. They spoke of the group's collegiality and encouraged me to attend a section meeting. I followed their advice. From the first meeting, I was hooked.

On September 16, 2011, I birthed my brainchild: Johansen Law Office. While scary, the freedom to create my ideal environment, accept my right-fit clients, and personally handle their cases elevated my professional life. This was it: the Big Opportunity. And I had created it for myself.

I built momentum, one step after another. A friend from law school, Meghan Eaves, was launching her own solo practice, and suggested that we share a prime location downtown. We'd have camaraderie and decreased overhead. We locked in a ninth-floor office on Fourth Avenue in Minneapolis. Before moving into our office, we met to share gold nuggets mined from the endless resources on starting a solo practice. We'd look up from our laptops and sit back, in awe of our own audacity. We were going to do it: launch solo practices right out of law school. *Amazing!*

This is the discipline piece. Conceiving the complete vision (your seaworthy vessel) too soon scatters your focus. Keep your attention on what comes next. That may mean gathering information to reveal the next step. Once a board materializes, you take it and nail it into place. Then you reach for the next board.

Keep at it, and before long your boat will be strong enough to hold you and your dreams.

3 DETERMINATION

This building process for a customized practice sounds simple, doesn't it? If we were robots analyzing the business environment for best practices and applying them, then it would be simple. We would have no attachment to outcomes (mere data). We'd integrate what we learned and just keep marching on until we achieved the desired result. But we're humans, not robots. We experience not only the joy and exhilaration that spurs us to keep going, but the frustration, discouragement, and fear that can stop us in our tracks.

When setbacks happen, you need the third factor, foundational to Drive and Discipline: Determination. It's your commitment to your practice. You must cement it. If it's shaky, then setbacks will rock your resolve, and may cause you to abandon your path. The already-built ships that do not belong to you may lure you away.

My commitment to my criminal-defense practice was tested from the moment I shared with others my decision to build my practice. I was a new lawyer, young, and female (the last two still apply). Others considered these factors a shortlist of my greatest obstacles to success.

I considered them to be nothing more than descriptors. They didn't foreclose me from being capable, tenacious, and business savvy. Others disagreed. And I learned to not care.

You must confront the defeatist messaging of others. If their perspective works its way into your thoughts and becomes part of your inner critic, you will sabotage yourself. Your entrepreneurial path will present enough challenges and obstacles. Don't put yourself on the list.

You'll find out early on if you have an inner critic. Doubt will appear in your internal narrative and attempt to dash your dreams. It's one of my inner critic's favorite forms. I remember the day Doubt appeared as a sledgehammer primed to swing. I had my office space. I'd created my firm, made it official with the state, and set its launch date: December 1, 2011.

And then it got real.

The voices of my real-life naysayers showed up as my own inner narrative: *Who do you think you are? You have to pay your dues! How are you going to get clients? Launching a firm right out of law school is a recipe for disas-*

ter! My naysayers had vocalized these questions aloud, but underlying their interrogation was the ultimate question, and none dared to ask it directly: What if you fail?

I mustered up the courage to ask myself the big question:

Oh my God . . . what if I fail?

It was as if these negative fears were somehow more grounded in reality than my dreams. I sat with my terror. Bile rose in my throat, my chest clenched, and my heart raced. I have so much to do! But I had a business plan, and a master to-do list. Never in my life had I shied away from hard work. I'd do the work, and do it well. I'd check off item by item. I agonized. *Why? Why am I putting myself through this terror, this uncertainty?* One thing I was sure of: these negative thoughts were not going to inspire me.

I found inspiration by focusing on the intention behind my endeavor: to help my future clients, to serve others. This focus obliterated my fear of failure—which I realized was rooted in concern for my ego and keeping it intact. Shifting my focus onto serving my future clients made my business no longer about me. And so my fears became irrelevant. All I knew was that I was willing to set sail with the goal of service, along with acceptance of the possibility of serving no one—willing to let the criminal-defense client pool decide if there was a need for me and my legal services.

I'm going for it!

Essentially, I committed to being true to my self in bringing my business vision to life—whatever happened. Even when it's hard—when others discourage me, or someone else's path appears easier to take. Even when I could not see the next step, I had the drive, discipline, and determination to make it materialize.

WHAT IS THE REASON BEHIND YOUR ENDEAVOR THAT RESONATES WITH YOUR CORE?

ARE YOU WILLING TO COMMIT TO BEING "TRUE TO YOU" IN BRINGING YOUR BUSINESS DREAM TO LIFE— NO MATTER WHAT?

PART II:
BRAND "YOU"

In Part I, we talked about unleashing your entrepreneurial spirit. You need Drive, Discipline, and Determination to bring your practice to life. Now, we'll delve into what you may encounter in the entrepreneurial ocean.

4 SHOW YOUR FACE

When I scanned the criminal-defense seascape, I observed that its "face" was middle-aged and male. This unvarying picture stared out relentlessly from advertising materials aimed at those accused of criminal conduct. Women did occasionally purchase advertising space, but were unwilling to show their faces. In a directory of criminal-defense attorneys, I found one photo of a female lawyer—in a small, black-and-white display ad.

I had committed to being true to me in bringing my business dream to life, regardless of the environment I'd entered. Here, that meant I'd be the face of my firm—even when I'd be the only female lawyer with a full-color advertisement. Into the sea of aggressive red ads featuring stern, middle-aged men splashed a young, female, smiling face set against a teal backdrop.

Not only did clients call me, they sighed in relief and made comments like this one: "Thank God you answered. You're my first choice. I just wanted to talk to another woman." And it wasn't just women opting to call me. Men, shaken by being thrust into jail as common criminals, chose to call someone who looked "friendly." First-timers (my right-fit clients) flocked to me. And all I'd done was show up, and present a different kind of face as an option.

I am willing to entertain a wide latitude on how a business gets built. "True to You" may mean something very different for you than for me. But I will not budge on this matter: you need to be the face of your business to attract your right-fit clients. You can always hide, but if you do, then you make it hard for your right-fit clients to find you and connect with you. You lose a credibility advantage, because you're not at the forefront, transparent and willing to be seen.

If you are willing to be seen, it means that you plaster your face all over your advertising materials. A photo draws the eye and creates an instant connection. It makes you human to viewers. They can look at your face and see if you're confident, approachable, and enjoy what you do. When they work with you, they're getting the owner—the face of the firm. Boom! Instant credibility.

When a viewer responds to your advertisement by calling you, she hears your voice and sees your face. Credibility builds and connection begins. You determine that this viewer is a potential right-fit client, and warmly invite her to meet for an initial consultation. She had already visualized who she wants as her lawyer—you. When she arrives at your office for the initial consultation, instead of watching each suit walk by wondering if it's you, her eyes light up in recognition when you enter the reception area. She knows you even before you shake hands for the first time. And she is seriously considering you for representation. Those other guys? Out of sight and out of mind.

Building brand loyalty to you, owner of your practice, begins at the first impression. Make it impactful.

5 SHATTER THE MOLD

Sometimes when you show up and shatter the mold, you'll encounter those who want to thwart your efforts. They're personally invested in the mold (they fit it), or at least they have no idea how to treat mold-breakers. The former will treat you like you don't belong on their turf, and the latter will treat you as deviant for not fulfilling your socially acceptable role.

Two weeks after my law-firm launch, my phone rang. I grabbed a pen and a yellow pad, trying not to seem overexcited and scare the caller off. (Nobody calling about a criminal case wants to think that you're thrilled about their situation.)

Summoning my most professional tone, I answered, "Law office, Rita speaking."

"Is Mr. Johansen there?" asked Sexism, channeled through a middle-aged woman.

"You realize that you've called Johansen Law Office?"

"Yes."

"No misters work here."

"Well, I want to speak to the person in charge." She maybe thought me an inept receptionist. "You are. I'm Rita Johansen."

She didn't miss a beat. "I'm with a shredding company you simply have to use. I have a salesman in your area. He'll drop in within the next half hour to work out an arrangement for you to use our services to shred your law firm's confidential papers."

I waited. She offered nothing else.

"Don't you think you should apologize for starting our conversation on the wrong foot?" *With the other one lodged in your mouth*, I thought.

"What do you mean?"

"You assumed that a law-firm owner must be a man. Now that you've discovered your error, don't you think an apology is in order?"

"No. My salesman will be there in half an hour. I'll make sure he calls you Miss Johansen. Have a good day."

"And I'll make sure to have a macho mister handy to toss him to the curb. I won't take his meeting. You've shredded any chance to do business with me. Don't call here again. Good day."

Of course her salesman never showed.

That's how I learned that the perpetrator of sexism can be female. The caller had assumed that I was merely the phone-answerer for Mr. Someone-Who-Fits-the-Mold, and after learning her error, made no attempt to applaud her sister-woman's efforts to change the face of criminal defense. After I hung up, I sat for a while, hanging my head, feeling betrayed. And then I realized it wasn't about me. Her beliefs about socially acceptable women's work had no bearing on me and my law firm's success. Her beliefs limited only her.

I reminded myself of my commitment to serve my clients—whatever happens. Even when a middle-aged woman assumes I am the secretary, not the business owner. I thought at first that this occurrence was a fluke, but my confidence was misplaced. This dismissive treatment kept happening to me (and my young, female colleagues).

Early on, I learned to wear suits, even at conferences where others wore business casual. Jeans were a luxury for middle-aged men. As a young female in jeans, I'd be mistaken for a legal secretary, a law student, a paralegal, a law clerk, or a court reporter. And the person who assumed I had a subordinate role instead of an ownership position would blame me for their mistake: I had "tricked" them by failing to fit the mold. They asked me to clarify a few times, as if convinced at any moment I would say, "Got you! A young, female criminal-defense solo practitioner? What a hoot! I answer phones for Mr. Johansen—the big boss." Had I given this reply, I would expect this response: "Now that makes sense." And we would laugh together uproariously at my ruse.

But that never happened, and I didn't find this dismissive treatment funny. I disagreed with its underlying premise: the claim I made (that I belonged in my ownership position in criminal defense) was absurd. And, through practice, I became better at confronting it. At a happy hour, a woman laughed when I told her I owned a criminal-defense law practice. She thought I was joking, but swallowed her laughter when she saw my quizzical brow. "But you don't look like a criminal-defense lawyer," she said, trying to save face.

To which I smiled and replied, "I'm well aware. My clients seem to really enjoy that fact. And they don't fit the stereotype for criminals. So we're well-suited to each other."

Soon after the Mr. Johansen paper-shredder phone call, I found myself in a nightclub surrounded by my fellow defenders who did fit the mold. A family lawyer, Jane Moore, had invited me to Charlie Calvino's Christmas party. She'd described this affair as one attended by "everyone who is anyone." I jumped at it. Three weeks into my practice, I had fresh business cards in my purse and was eager to be someone.

Jane took the lead, scanning the low-lit lounge for a good starting place before settling on a cocktail table encircled by middle-aged men with slicked-back hair and a used-car-salesman vibe. I knew their practice area even before she told me: criminal defense.

"This is my friend Rita Johansen," Jane said. "She just launched a criminal-defense firm."

"Pleased to meet you, Sweetie," one said. He looked me over from head to toe, stopping in the middle, and sucked his teeth.

"Hi." I waited for his eyes to travel back to my face. "Maybe you didn't catch my name. It's Rita. Rita Johansen." I moved past him to his mirror image.

"Hi, Beautiful," said the clone, grinning in his blatant disregard for my true identity.

I made the request again. "Hi. And it's Rita, not 'Beautiful.'"

"Well, you're certainly beautiful."

"Well, you're certainly slick."

The third lookalike broke in. "What's a pretty thing like you doing defending criminals?"

"Same as you, I'd imagine. See you in court."

Jane and I wound our way to the next table for more introductions. After the first leering gaze at my legs, I wished I'd worn a pantsuit instead of a skirt and jacket. I applauded myself for staying calm and cool as I faced sexism in the flesh. I couldn't help but think that these men were watching to see if I'd crack under their objectification.

I called it an early night and returned to my office to analyze the situation. My examination led me to clarify my position in my marketplace, and the essence of my brand. I started here: As a student prosecutor at the Hennepin County Attorney's Office, I had been treated as a legal professional. I'd entered criminal-defense practice thinking that my gender would have no impact on my treatment as a business owner—not in 2011. Wrong! Slumping in my office chair, I thought, *What can I do about their behavior? How do I convince them that I'm serious about my practice? How do I make them see me as an equal, not a "pretty thing?" How can I fit in with these "big names" in Minneapolis criminal defense?*

Even after great amounts of careful planning, nothing elucidates the seascape like setting sail. That night, the sea seemed tumultuous and murky. I had not realized that I'd charted a course into the epicenter of the Good Old Boys Club (GOBC). And it had reared up as a sea monster thrashing giant tentacles. I felt lost, out of place, alone. I had to figure out how to navigate my way out of this Bermuda Triangle. Or I'd sink.

The best way to diminish the power of a fearsome thing is to face it. Here were the facts: The GOBC had failed to welcome me into their criminal-defense clique. They were right; I did not belong in it. Only by betraying myself could I fit in. I'd have to join in the degrading banter and exchange got-her-off-this, got-him-out-of-that stories. I'd have to treat my practice as egocentric, not client-centered.

I mentally put on their ill-fitting, man-sized shoes and walked around for a while to better understand them. What had society told them about how they could become worthy, prestigious, and admirable? What attributes did they possess? What's their ideal image? How do they work with their clients—particularly women? What markers were on their barometer for success? What were the benefits of this approach? The shortcomings?

After I experienced the appalling way Mr. Defender treated me—as a criminal-defense colleague —I wondered how he would have treated me as a client. I played out this scenario in my mind's eye. He pulled up in front of my mental courthouse in his black beamer. His smile and suit were both flashy. Once he roared onto the scene, I wouldn't have to worry my pretty little head. He'd take care of everything. I had one job: look pretty. He'd lavish me with compliments on my beauty, because that's what matters most to women—their appearance. Leave the tough mental stuff to the guys, he'd instruct me. In reply, I'd giggle and fan myself in relief. Maybe even bat my eyelashes. All the better to induce the menfolk to roll up their shirtsleeves to tackle my indelicate legal situation.

He's successful when he puts on a big show at trial and tallies another win. His record is measured in trial victories. When he meets potential clients, he leads with this tally, segues into war stories, and ends by assuring them that he's handled cases like theirs dozens, if not hundreds, of times.

Mr. Defender's approach, while impressive, has many disadvantages. Effectively guiding a woman through the legal system requires much more than a wink, a kiss on the hand, and instructions not to worry her pretty little head. And Mr. Defender's expectations for the case (a flashy trial or a quick plea) may be the opposite of what his client really needs (a negotiated resolution). He makes assumptions about his client's expectations and builds his case strategy around them. His client is a passive spectator at the Mr. Defender Show. Please stay seated, Sweetie, and don't bother me with too many questions.

Prior to my law firm launch, I had thought the Mr. Defender stereotype persisted only on- screen. I made these assumptions: real-life defenders did not demean and dismiss women, and they weren't the alter ego of their clients. Criminal defense couldn't be that bad, could it? Before launching my practice, I knew no criminal defenders, and many ethical, emotionally intelligent prosecutors. I figured my new colleagues would be like my old, except they'd sit at the counsel table on the other side of the aisle. But then I met Mr. Defender in real life, multiplied to fill a Minneapolis nightclub. We've failed to shatter the mold as a society, and it keeps churning out Mr. Defenders that make criminal defense a cesspool. A fellow defender summed up his approach to his practice as follows: "Anything short of smoking meth with your client goes."

I had to decide right there, in the captain's chair, how to handle this development. Would I abandon my ship? NO! I resolved to chart a new course. I'd practice criminal defense differently. It wasn't about puffery and appearances, bragging, and showmanship; it wasn't about fitting the Mr. Defender mold or acceptance by the GOBC. My practice would center on helping my clients. And this would make all the difference. My strong brand, my niche, my marketing, my relationships—all grew organically from this decision to create a new model for a criminal-defense firm, centered on staying true to who I am.

Some clients do prefer the Mr. Defender model. Often, they're veterans of the legal system. In contrast, my right-fit client was a first-timer who needed extensive education and emotional support along with competent legal counsel. That's the beauty of the True to You Approach. There's room in the courtroom for attorneys like me, and for attorneys like Mr. Defender (and across the spectrum). Mr. Defender would serve my right-fit client poorly; and Mr. Defender's right-fit client would be a poor fit for my law firm.

Sometimes, who you are sets you apart from your competitors. They see you in court and that cues them in that you're attracting clients. Because they believe you invaded their turf, they rear up and defend their paradigm for their practice area by offending you—to scare you off so you stop stealing their clients. That must be what is happening, in their minds. How else could a lawyer right out of law school have such a client list? They don't understand that their dismissive and degrading behavior repels the same potential clients that your emotionally intelligent practice magnetizes. Mr. Defenders' sexist behavior was my big "come what may" to rise above. By focusing on what this new development meant for serving my right-fit clients, I spotted my greatest competitive advantage: emotional intelligence. And I discovered a wonderful commonality with my right-fit clients: We both shattered the mold. They weren't your stereotypical "criminals," and I wasn't a Mr. Defender.

To frame my environment in supply-demand terms, an abundance of Mr. Defenders in a stormy sea compels those who fit the Mr. Defender mold to compete pirate-style for clientele. Aargh! But there was only one Rita Johansen, anchored in a placid lagoon of emotionally intelligent defenders, and many potential clients who, when given the choice (because I showed my "face" as another option), elected to head for the lagoon. Instead of raising the white flag of defeat or the red skull-and-crossbones of a Mr. Defender, I hoisted the Johansen Law Office pennant. It was teal.

Dare to stand out. In my experience, it's the best way to claim your niche in your marketplace.

6 STAY SOLO, OR
PARTNER WITH CARE

I took the advice so commonplace in the business world: find a mentor. And so I set out to locate an experienced criminal-defense attorney who would treat me as an equal, not an ornamental object. Three weeks after Calvino's Christmas party, I visited Jeremiah Wilson, a real-estate lawyer, for website advice. "Richard Banner has a fantastic website," Jeremiah said. "By the way, he's a criminal- defense lawyer." Jeremiah gave me Banner's email address.

Two days later, Banner and I met for lunch. He told me he planned to take a year off from the law due to burnout, and didn't see it as a threat to his business to help me with mine. I officially asked. He accepted. Bam! I had a formal criminal-defense mentor.

Four weeks after this lunch, Banner breezed into my conference room and said, "This hit me on the elevator ride up. We should partner together. Just hear me out. I wouldn't have it any other way than fifty-fifty."

I stared at him, dumbfounded.

"You know, even though I have more experience and an established practice, I would want everything equal. You can even have top billing. Johansen-Banner."

"Thank you for the opportunity. I'll consider it when you go back to practicing law in a year. Let's see how we work together in the meantime."

"I think I'll return sooner than that. Start giving it some thought. Think about your reservations."

Why is this even on the table? I thought. *Why does he want to convert his one-man show into a two-attorney operation with a lawyer he's known for only a month? Maybe I'm just that impressive. Or what appeals to him most is my firm's bank account.* My gut clenched.

After one week, Banner called me with an announcement.

"I'm going back to practicing law. You know, there's a lot we have to hash out before partnering. Like, I want to meet my potential partner's family."

"Whoa! Back up. When did that happen?"

"This morning. Let's focus on the future. I'm back in the game! Have you thought about partnering? Like I said, I wanna meet my potential partner's family.

You know."

A silent moment stretched on while my gut urged me to decline his invite on the spot. I resisted, opting to do reconnaissance. "No, I don't. Maybe you could explain it a bit more. Why? Why meet my family?"

"Because partnership is like a marriage."

"Have you ever been married?"

"Actually, I have. We parted amicably enough. I think if we're going to take the big step of partnering, we should know each other very well. Maybe that's the wrong analogy."

"Yeah, I can imagine my husband's reaction to my telling him you want to marry me, but don't worry, it's strictly in a business sense." I managed to swallow my laughter, but it stayed close to the surface. Though he sounded animated, I knew he was serious. "You're right," I said. "It's a big step. We should know each other better. Let's table this."

"You know, I'm serious about the top billing, even though I have more experience than you."

"It isn't about top billing. I started a solo practice on purpose. Let's just keep working together. Table the partnership idea."

"Okay. In the meantime, you should come up with a list of your reservations, your concerns."

"That's fair. To even make that list, I'd have to get to know you better, see how you work on cases. So let's revisit this in, say, six months."

"I don't know about six months. That seems a little long."

"Then let's agree to table it indefinitely."

"Sure, but I feel very strongly we met for a reason. You know, I was starting to get burned out from the law. It helps to have your enthusiasm about it."

"It's helped to have your practical pointers. Win-win. Now, let's talk about this case."

I was eager to change the subject back to work and away from these awkward ideas of meeting my family and getting to know me better on a personal level. I wanted a strictly professional mentor. He'd felt isolated in his solo practice, but I wasn't the one to chase away his loneliness.

As a new lawyer, I'd thought I needed a seasoned mentor in my practice area. And Banner didn't call me Sugar, Honey, Sweetie, or tell me I was too pretty to defend criminals; he championed me. But my gut signaled he wasn't a suitable business partner. And I had told him the truth. I'd started a solo practice on purpose.

This happens to other startup solo practitioners—the premature invitation from a seasoned solo practitioner to partner. It's difficult to discern the motives behind this invite. They may be noble: your work ethic, business savvy, and representation style are impressive. Or they may be sketchy: your firm's bank account appeals, your strong work ethic means you will work your ass off while your "partner" gives his bare two cents.

If you receive such an invitation, I'd suggest formally associating on a case first. You will have a great vantage point to collect insight on how your prospective partner engages in representation. I associated with my prospective partner on a case and learned the following: he was strapped for cash, not business savvy, and unethical. Banner had a worse handle on the law than I did, and encouraged me to do the bulk of the work (to "gain experience," he said). In the end, Banner did not work hard enough to earn his half of the shared fee. And I ended up having to take steps to protect the integrity of our shared client's case when Banner engaged in unethical behavior.

My gut was right. He was not a suitable business partner. A fifty-fifty split and top billing with a more experienced criminal defender like Banner would have knocked me off course for establishing an emotionally intelligent, ethical law firm. Stay solo, or partner with care.

7 PROTECT YOUR PRACTICE

I ended up with various metaphors for the environment in criminal defense that has been created by the majority, the Good Old Boys Club of Mr. Defenders—stormy seas, a cesspool, a pigpen. To stay true to me, I minimized contact with the GOBC and focused on making my practice a serene sanctuary for those seeking an emotionally intelligent representative. Calvino's Christmas party had been enough exposure; I did not want to muddy myself (and dirty my brand) by playing in the criminal-defense muck. And so I resolved to keep my brand clean by avoiding associations with the GOBC. Or so I thought I was doing—until Banner made a mess in my office.

I introduced Richard Banner to Meghan Eaves, my officemate. He started the conversation by pointing to Meghan's computer screen that was displaying her friend's social medial page and asking Meghan if the woman on the screen was single. Banner then made sexist jokes using slang for female genitalia—in my office, to my officemate.

"I hate that word," she snapped.

Banner grinned, bent down to get in Meghan's face, and said, "Crotch, crotch, crotch, crotch, crotch, crotch, crotch."

Meghan looked over at me, eyebrows raised as if he'd slapped her. She was primed to punch him, but she held back.

I led him away from Meghan and into the conference room. "Rick, when you visit my office, please don't use words like 'crotch.' It's not appropriate. It's offensive."

Banner flared up. "It's not my fault she can't take a joke. That she has a crotch issue." He laughed, but stopped when he noticed my glower. "She doesn't have a sense of humor. I don't waste my time with oversensitive people who can't take a joke. I'm used to talking with criminal-defense guys where this is the sense of humor. I'm going to say whatever I wanna say, whenever I wanna say it, wherever, to whoever!" His grin returned, infuriatingly.

Oh, the luxury of membership in the Good Old Boys Club: the power to offend anyone, at any time, in any place, and to do so without any apology. I wanted to kick Banner to the curb, but we were associating on an open case. I had a duty to my client to continue working with him. "I'm not banning you from telling sex jokes about women. That's not in my power. But don't do it in my office. I'm not one of the guys. I'm a lady lawyer. So is Meghan. If you can't abide by that, we can meet elsewhere."

"Maybe I'm not used to working with women. I'll try to be better about it."

"Thanks. That's all I ask."

Banner had worked with women for years. He'd had many female clients and encountered female associates, court personnel, and other women in the justice system. Through it all, he'd remained ignorant of the degrading nature of his behavior, due to a failure of leadership. When I spoke up as a leader, it shocked him. As a business owner demanding appropriate behavior in my law office, I was harder to dismiss than the women he'd joked about. And so he paid attention. He changed his behavior at my request.

You can remove yourself from a mucky environment and choose your associations. Granted, people are most often on their best behavior, but they occasionally lapse. And when they do, you are free to betray yourself (and smudge your brand) by not saying anything. Or you can speak up. You are your brand. Protect its integrity.

Business ownership came with a responsibility I hadn't considered prior to my law-firm launch, because I hadn't expected a sexist environment. Every business owner is a leader responsible for protecting the integrity of their business and their profession. The GOBC didn't sanction me to speak out against their behavior. As their equal, I sanctioned my own speech, knowing that what they did with my words was outside of my control. I couldn't make them stop. But every time I interrupted this banter, they clammed up and glared, or changed topics. When you have the power to speak (and as a leader, you do), use it to empower others. It's the right thing to do.

Often, you do something because it is right, but it turns out to also be good for business. I am female-friendly and willing to be seen as such. I'd speak out when I heard sexist banter in court. On one occasion, a Mr. Defender asked, "Who do you think you are?"

I replied, "I'm Rita Johansen of Johansen Law Office." A woman in the galley called me later that day to discuss representation. To the GOBC, I was an outcast; to women-lovers and the emotionally intelligent, I was a safe haven.

8 YOUNG, FEMALE, AND PHENOMENAL

I find it disgusting and disgraceful that women still face sexism when they set out to do business. Enough obstacles and struggles exist in the business world; sexism should not be one of them. We have to shine light on it, or sexism will continue to spread like black mold. It's hard to breathe it in and continue to rise, but this is precisely what I did in my legal practice. And I did not do it in isolation.

Knowing I could not have comradeship with those seeking to objectify me, I found collegiality elsewhere, outside the criminal-defense cesspool. My officemate and I created our own affinity group for young, female solo practitioners. Had we not dared to share our stories with each other, we'd have missed out on the wonderful friendships formed and the cathartic connections that took place at our get-togethers.

And I found a fabulous champion, Lauren De-Vries. Her office is splashed with bold print; her brand color is pink. She said, "Put on your stilettos, Miss Rita, and prance into that courtroom." She invited me to call her if I ever needed any encouragement to do so.

I love the sentiment behind this message: You're worthy of showing up, and being seen. Female does not equal unprofessional; it equals phenomenal. Make way for phenomenal in the courtroom. And so I strode into each court hearing, head held high, wearing heels and remembering, as I observed the GOBC members clustered around defense counsel table, that I had a place in that courtroom, too.

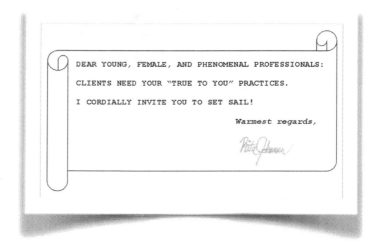

DEAR YOUNG, FEMALE, AND PHENOMENAL PROFESSIONALS:

CLIENTS NEED YOUR "TRUE TO YOU" PRACTICES.

I CORDIALLY INVITE YOU TO SET SAIL!

Warmest regards,

PART III:
CHAMPION
RELATIONSHIPS

9 RELATIONSHIP BUILDING
(NOT NETWORKING)

**FIVE (5) GUIDELINES FOR
MAXIMUM IMPACT:**

1. DEVELOP AN ABUNDANCE MENTALITY
2. ENVISION YOUR RIGHT-FIT CLIENTS
3. MAKE MEANINGFUL CONNECTIONS
4. ASK FOR YOUR RIGHT-FIT CLIENTS
5. GO OUTSIDE YOUR PROFESSION

MAX IMPACT MARKERS:

MEMORABLE IMPRESSIONS
MEANINGFUL RELATIONSHIPS
MEATY CASES, NOT SCRAPS

You will have many opportunities to reach out to others about your business. Networking events are touted as the be-all, end-all of business building. They have become formulaic and stilted. What leads to tense, awkward interactions at networking events? The smiles that don't reach eyes. Many networkers believe the myth that they must leave their humanity at the door. They enter, cloaked in their cool, collected, and controlled professional personas.

When we cross the threshold as our true selves, we build real, meaningful relationships, because it's in our nature as humans to connect about what enthuses and inspires us. And these relationships turn out to be good for business. Follow the five guidelines below to use relationship-building opportunities to have the 3M Impact: make memorable impressions, cultivate meaningful relationships, and attract meaty cases, not scraps.

Guideline #1:
Develop an abundance mentality.

Many solo practitioners operate from a scarcity mentality, and it shows up in their practice; their right-fit clients are scarce. I went to a solo- and small-firm conference, attended by other entrepreneurs who had done it: leapt into the fray. They were joyous and enthusiastic, right? Wrong.

I sat at a long table and looked to either side of me, smiling and trying to make eye contact to strike up a conversation. Nothing. My colleagues kept their heads down, frowns in place and eyes focused on their screens.

The scheduled seminar topic was data security, but it devolved into discussion about how a legal website was "stealing our business." We faced grave external threats to our livelihood: hackers were seeking to breach our security measures, and this website was encroaching on our turf, making the client pool ever smaller.

An anxious state of mind does not serve you or your business. It's one thing to plan for disaster. Take reasonable measures to do so. But do not operate in an anxiety-ridden state. Nobody is drawn to these emotions or to the actions that come from this mental frenzy. (See Time for Self in Part IV for tips on unwinding and de-stressing naturally.) On the other hand, when you are deeply rooted to your own sense of self, the power you possess, and the unique talents you offer, you are secure in your place within your profession.

Develop an abundance mentality, and your positive approach will show up whenever you have a chance to connect with others about your business, as it did for me. I loved my practice. Why wouldn't I? I designed my days, and served my right-fit clients. And I was open about my joy. Often, I heard how my colleagues were surviving. "I'm hanging in there," they'd say. Or they'd be the victims of circumstance. "I'm getting battered by this tough economy." Who was this downright cheerful woman who showed up to events wearing a suit and a smile? Me. If you are obviously enjoying what you do, people will be more likely to refer clients your way.

Maybe this advice triggers these thoughts: But I'd be faking it. I don't like what I do. My response: Why are you doing this to yourself? You get to design your business. Go back to the Drive discussion in Part I. Make your business into something that fills you with enthusiasm. That way, you're sharing with others, not fooling them. Build your practice around doing what you love. Share it with others, and your positive approach will attract clients.

Guideline #2:
Get clear on your right-fit clients.

The first guideline focused on your willingness to share your beloved endeavor with others. Your positive approach at networking events will attract referrals. Now, we'll fine-tune the message you send about whom you find it rewarding to serve: your right-fit clients.

Envision your right-fit client. Spend time thinking about these questions: Who do you want to walk through your door? Who do you best serve? What is your right-fit client's level of experience with your practice area? And then approach your analysis from the other side: Who would be a poor fit for your firm?

I wanted to serve new entrants into the criminal justice system who saw themselves as community members, not criminals. Hope still lit their eyes. On the flip side, misfit clients were jaded by the system. Their eyes lacked a spark. They'd ask me to do the unethical.

My vision for my right-fit client incorporated what I'd learned about my marketplace and my competitive advantage. I focused on my competencies and who I best served because of them. My analysis guided me to craft this client request: "I do strictly criminal defense. I most enjoy helping individuals thrust into the criminal justice system for the first time." I cast a net large enough to include my right-fit clients, and small enough to avoid capturing misfit clients.

Guideline #3:
Make meaningful connections.

It's meet-and-greet time. You can be the butterfly that flits around the room, scattering her business cards. For example, Janet shook hands, smiled, and said, "Hi, I'm Janet. Here's my card. Find me on social media. I'm on every site." Then she moved on to the next person. She was friendly, and that was good, but not memorable. People remember those with whom they connect in a meaningful way. To this very day, Janet's business card sits in many drawers, forgotten. Or maybe Janet became a social-media connection with the 300+ other butterflies from networking events.

When asked to give a referral, no one wants to say, "Let me rifle through my business-card stacks." Or, "Let me check my online connections." Instead, you're after this reply: "I know Rita Johansen from Minnesota Women Lawyers. I'll get you her number." This reflects reality—referral sources offer the first person who comes to mind. Thus, memorable people get priority for referrals. Janet's business card and her existence as a social-media connection amounted to nothing. Stacks of cards and social media are last-resort references when no one memorable comes to mind as a referral.

Pick a few affinity groups and organizations that you enjoy, and show up consistently. Better than making it your mission to get as many cards out as possible is to make meaningful connections. Relationship building is not about puffery, appearances, and trickery. Genuine interest in those you meet, enthusiasm about what you do, and being your authentic self will make you memorable. You don't need to be a big, bad legal personality and showcase yourself to the room. Engage in conversations one-on-one, if that's true to you. Let them see you light up about the business you're building around who you are. Trade business cards after you establish a connection. And have your photo on your business card. Instead of your new friend wondering later which card to set aside from the stack, she sees your smiling face. People often remember faces better than names.

Guideline #4: Ask for your right-fit clients.

The worst mistake practice owners make is that they fail to ask for their right-fit clients. You will hear this question: "What do you do?" I've heard variations on this common response: "A little real estate, some family." No! You don't do a little of this, of that, and some other things. You're not willing to accept as a client anyone who walks in your door. You may wonder what's wrong with this approach. The answer: it's haphazard. You're leaving it to chance that a right-fit client will come through your door. Chance is not a reliable way to grow your practice!

Ponder this scenario. I have a beagle, Lexus, whose mission in life is to obtain table scraps. At dinnertime, she sits within view and hopes that my husband and I will respond to the gleaming desire in her eyes by throwing her a few table scraps. We resist—well, almost always.

One day Lexus refused to settle for this measly fare, engaged in creative thinking, and tried a new approach. My husband and I, unaware of our dog's scheme, sat eating pizza at the island counter in our basement. Lexus had observed her humans' routine. Pizza night meant company was coming at some point. She would bark to signal their arrival. So bark she did. We clueless humans went upstairs to greet our friends. No one was at the front door.

And Lexus had disappeared.

She'd slunk downstairs, pushed out a bar stool, and boosted herself onto the countertop to devour half the meat-lover's pizza—her favorite people food.

I tell you this tale to emphasize the importance of not waiting for scraps; rather, business owners must home in on the type of cases they want. Obtaining referrals for right-fit clients does not require the trickery employed by my beagle; it requires planning, and a willingness to ask for what you truly want. Ask for a meaty case that you can really sink your teeth into.

New solo practitioners attend networking events and politely ask for any case, in any practice area. Seasoned attorneys will respond to the desire gleaming in their eyes and toss them a scrap. A scrap case is too minor to interest the seasoned attorney: the potential client is unable to pay a market-rate fee, or the seasoned lawyer has already flagged the potential client as a problem. Unaware there's another way to feed her neophyte law practice, the rookie networker gobbles up this scrap case, and then waits for the next tidbit to fall. You cannot build a law practice on scraps. Like associates with like; scraps refer other scrap cases, and your practice will slowly starve to death.

Along with scrap cases, you will receive a reputation in the legal community as a bottom-feeder. You may kid yourself: you'll work your way up from small cases with unqualified clients to big cases with your right-fit clients. But this misguided notion does not reflect reality. These scrap cases will fail to generate the income necessary to keep your doors open. And no one is monitoring you to determine that you did well on a scrap case and have earned a meatier case. You're the boss, not an associate spoon-fed cases by ownership. You'd become known as the Scrap Lawyer. Because you would have done such a great job on your scrap case, your former scrap client or another referral source would give you a reward: a referral for another scrap case.

Whenever someone asks you about what you do, make your right-fit client request. Here's mine: "I do strictly criminal defense. And I most enjoy helping individuals thrust into the criminal justice system for the first time." When an individual who fits your description asks your referral source for a recommendation, you're bumped to the front of the line, because you were enthusiastic, memorable, and specific.

Guideline #5: Go outside your profession.

My community consists of many non-lawyers. Remembering what it was like to not know any lawyers, I wanted to bridge this gap. I let everyone know that I was happy to make connections if anyone needed a lawyer.

My non-lawyer community members would ask: Do you know any real-estate lawyers? Have you come across any family lawyers you trust? I'd either supply contact information for an attorney I trusted in that practice area, or ask my lawyer friends for referral ideas. What message did this send to my non-legal community members? I'm engaged with my colleagues in the legal community, and care about helping people find quality legal assistance. It also helped my non-legal community members to transition from thinking of me as pre-law-practice Rita to criminal-defense lawyer Rita Johansen of Johansen Law Office. I had an informal attorney-referral service going, and charged nothing for it. It was the right thing to do to help my community.

It turned out to be good for business. If Uncle John's buddy had "a few too many" on the golf course and failed to drive home safely, what criminal-defense lawyer came to mind? The marketing term for these contacts is *impressions*. The more impressions others have of your business (meaning you, because you are your brand), the more likely they are to remember you when they need you. Impressions go beyond the effect of your print advertisement or a visit to your website. It includes things like your enthusiastic mentions of service to your right-fit clients. I'd say, "I took on a new case today—another first-timer to the system. It's so rewarding to guide her through the process." You impress upon those who show an interest in what you do that you are enthusiastic, selective, and dedicated to your work. Why wouldn't you be? You're bringing the practice of your dreams to life in the way that is true to you. Share it with your community members outside your profession.

10 NAYSAYERS ARE INSIGNIFICANT

Naysayers will send this message: you're doomed to fail at your endeavor. My most vocal naysayers were among my flock of family and friends. When I shared my plan to launch my practice, they revealed themselves as wolves in sheep's clothing. They'd say, "It's your life," seeming to be kind by relinquishing control over my life to its rightful owner. And then they'd continue.

- "I just don't think you really know what you're getting yourself into." (Despite their having done nothing close to what I intended to do, somehow they knew better than I what it was really about.)
- "I just don't think you're cut out for that."
- "I just know how hard it is to make it doing

that." (Yet they'd done nothing similar.)

- "I just don't want you to get hurt." (Many view failure as the ultimately painful experience that knocks a person down for the count. They forget about the rise.)
- "I just think you're better suited to something else." (Bring me another dream and I'll stomp on that one, too.)
- "I just know it's not realistic."
- "I just know it's not practical."
- "I just know you won't make any money at it."

My naysayers believed they were fortune tellers. Unless I followed their chosen path, my future looked bleak.

I started to cringe at "I just," knowing what would inevitably follow, and took it personally, at first. Didn't they know what I was capable of? Sure, I hadn't launched a law practice—*yet*. They assumed I did not have it in me to build a successful solo criminal-defense practice. Their lack of faith hurt me. They were "shoulding" all over me. And I refused to suffocate under a pile of "shoulds."

Then I realized that their reactions had nothing to do with me. They were projecting their fears. A theme popped up: my most vocal naysayers were middle-aged women who'd had their own dreams but had squashed them to pay their dues. They hadn't given themselves permission to do what they loved. Why would they give me the green light to bring my dreams to life? They flashed red; acted as though, if I kept going, I'd drive off a cliff; and they moaned and wailed about my impending demise. To satisfy them, I would have had to make a U-turn and exit onto the roadway that they deemed safe.

I tried to better understand these women. At eighteen, they had felt so old. When they'd moved past it, as the years had flashed by, they'd yearned for eighteen: the age to play around, to discover, to be bold— before debt, grown-up work, and family commitments had tied them down. Then they'd decided it was impossible to take risks. Having let their inner fears gobble up their dreams like wolves in sheep's clothing, they took the safe route. They became their own greatest limiters, putting everyone else first, taking on more commitments—not stopping to cultivate their talents, not daring to build their lives around doing what they loved. They edged their true selves out.

In their path came this twenty-five-year-old fresh from law school who said that she'd launch a law firm and succeed. She had the audacity to believe she could do it without paying her dues. Who did she think she was? She wasn't special. She couldn't take the easy way to the top while they'd worked damn hard for decades to get where they were. How was she going to get clients? What made her think she could start a business when she'd never done it before? These were the questions they voiced. But I could intuit the unsaid, and what they most wanted to know: What if she fails? Like a dirty four-letter word, fail was not mentioned to me by even one of them. They attached immense shame and unworthiness to failure.

I'd held my dream close to my chest for fear it'd be stomped on. When I'd trusted them with it, I expected them to apply fertilizer. Instead, they sprayed poison onto it, hoping it'd die—for my own good. They hoped that I'd take the safe route and realize I had to wait for someone else to give me an opportunity.

These women had nurtured, instead of challenged, their inner critics. They had a well-rehearsed inner dialogue about why they themselves could not go after the dreams they held near and dear to their hearts. And so they were ready with the language meant to shove me into the box that they had put themselves in, and to keep me there—where it was safe. I appreciate that their intentions were noble. They wanted to protect me from disappointment, difficulty, and uncertainty.

One of my favorite childhood activities was to hide (inside of clothing racks, in closets), and then wait until my target approached. I'd burst out and yell, "Surprise!" Then I'd clutch my stomach and scream with laughter. Surprises thrilled me. A while passed before I caught on that some people find uncertainty terrifying. I thought about this when deciding how to handle the naysayers in my life. What were my options? I could take the route that they deemed safe and stuff down my dreams. But then I'd be stifling my entrepreneurial spirit. I made the decision that was true to me.

The best way to demonstrate that I never belonged in the box they'd tried to guide me into (that existed only in their minds) was to bring my vision for my law firm to life. Any attempt to explain why they were lying to themselves about my limitations (and their own) would fall on deaf ears. They had trusted their inner critics for decades. Maybe they'd see me succeed, and this would lead them to question their fear-based narrative. But I was not responsible for their lives; I was responsible for mine. And I refused to give my power away. After my naysayers revealed themselves, I stopped seeking out their opinions. And I dismissed their unsolicited "guidance" as insignificant.

I must make myself very clear here. Why was the naysayers' advice insignificant? Never having set sail in their own ocean, they based their criticisms on nothing but fear. So instead of paying attention to my naysayers, I went out to seek champions.

WHEN OTHERS SHOVE YOU IN A TIDY BOX
BE BOLD ENOUGH TO UNAPOLOGETICALLY
BURST OUT,
GRINNING
AS A COLORFUL JANE-IN-THE-BOX.

FOR YOU KNEW THE SECRET:
IT WAS ONLY A MATTER OF TIME
BEFORE YOU BROKE FREE.

ALIGN WITH THOSE WHO REACT IN
DELIGHT,
NOT FRIGHT OR ANGER,
AT YOUR ESCAPE.

11 CULTIVATE A COMMUNITY OF CHAMPIONS

Your time and your energy are your most precious resources. Your relationships will reflect how you spend them. Spend them on champions, not naysayers.

A champion respects your vision for your life, helps you to amplify and gain clarity on your vision, and offers assistance in manifesting it. You will know when you meet a champion. This person will acknowledge how you light up when you talk about your endeavor, and will inquire about it. A champion will offer concrete ways to assist you.

Pay attention when champions show up in your life. Make an effort to cultivate these relationships. They will energize and enthuse you. Instead of stomping on your flowering dream, they will fertilize it and help you to tend to it. And they will celebrate with you when it blooms into a garden of splendor.

Show up for your champions. When you put in the time, pay attention, engage, and share your true self, the result is a close relationship. If instead you offer sparse face time (your actual face), shoot off only an occasional email, ignore what matters to your potential champion, or share only your puffed-up self, then you will have someone who may give you good advice (a mentor), but isn't invested in your success (a champion). People offer more thoughtful, creative, and tailored assistance to those with whom they have a close relationship.

The day after my law firm launch, one of my champions referred a case my way. To me, it was epic: Johansen Law Office's first client, Rita Johansen's first case as a criminal-defense solo practitioner. It nudged aside the pending United States Supreme Court cases in importance. With it, my champion gave me the best grand-opening present: her confidence in me. Your champions will show up for you, as you have shown up for them.

12 MAKE THE CASA ASK

THE CASA ASK™

1. GET CLEAR
2. POSITIVE ATTITUDE
3. BE SPECIFIC
4. BE APPRECIATIVE

The CASA Ask is a four-step process to invite your champions to help you bring your business vision to life. As a solo practitioner, I knew I'd limit my practice's potential to grow if I restricted my resources to my own skills and experience. And that's also a lonely way to build a solo practice. So I cultivated relationships with champions and shared my endeavor with them. I asked for help, jumped over hazards, and took shortcuts to success by listening to my champions' mistakes and practical pointers. I put their insights into action and implemented tried-and-true best practices.

The steps to the CASA Ask are straightforward. First, gain clarity on what you need. Do your due diligence on the problem. If it's something you can solve yourself, do not waste your champion's time. They're not a replacement for looking up case information or for reading and analyzing the case law that applies to your client's legal situation. (I hear this pet peeve from practitioners.) They're also not the ultimate decision-maker over your firm; never put that onus on a champion. Use their assistance to leapfrog ahead—implement best practices from your firm's inception. That's exciting for them, and for you. Don't abuse it to be lazy or to shirk your responsibilities.

Frame your ask in a positive light. Maybe your ask involves digitizing your records, implementing a new case-management system, or using a client-satisfaction survey. Whatever your ask, ultimately, you seek to better serve your clients. Share your noble intention with your champion.

Sometimes, the third step, be specific, is a sticking point. Your ask may require you to show vulnerability. Admit that you do not have all the answers. Yes, you have an inspired vision, and a commitment to bringing it to life. You'll find as you start building that you need more tools. You'll share your process, and learn that there's a better technique.

In these situations, be vulnerable, and brave. Bravery is not hunkering down and pretending all is well; it is admitting to the truth of a situation (like the mucky criminal-defense environment), and doing what it takes to rise above it. When you reveal the true status of your endeavor, you allow others to spot what you need to move forward. You can be vulnerable, admit you're not all-knowing and bulletproof, and still be seen as capable and strong.

When you tell your champions that you need help, they won't respond like your naysayers and sound the alarm: "See! This means you'll f— f— I can't even say it. It's too terrible. I told you so! You should have listened to me." Instead, your champions will express their confidence in you and even roll up their sleeves and grab a hammer. Whether it's insight, assistance, or support—it all helps the entrepreneur to keep going.

Early on, I expressed a fear to a champion: What if I made a mistake? Operating in perfectionist mode, I agonized and triple-checked. I needed insight on what the real-life consequences would be for making a mistake; my imagined consequences were mightily terrifying. My champion laughed, because she'd been there, and knew how to guide me through it. She had made a mistake in a case, and eventually landed in front of the Minnesota Supreme Court. She conceded her mistake, and argued that legal precedent still supported a finding in favor of her client. How did the prestigious panel of justices react to her concession? One said, "And that, Counselor, is why it is called the *practice* of law." She owned her mistake, moved past it, created a workaround, and her persistence was rewarded with a win for her client.

I had thought perfection was required of legal practitioners. A mistake would mean disgrace and public flogging. She gave me the perspective that a mistake is manageable. Lawyers are human. Although not anyone's ideal scenario, mistakes happen. When they do, the important thing is candor, and not letting it destroy your confidence in your abilities. My fear had taken up my most precious resources: energy and time. And my champion helped me to move past it.

Champions are excellent at helping you to banish your fears. You will never be fearless—but that's not what is required to grow your practice. Courage and fear coexist. You'll alternate between thrilled and terrified. That's not to say that you shouldn't face your fears. Because if you can shrink them, that's more time and energy you get to spend on being brave—

and that's when magnificence happens.

The final step is to show your appreciation after a champion helps you to better serve your right-fit clients. A quick post on social media is the least you can do, and your champion is aware of that. A phone call is better. Your champion can hear the appreciation in your voice. I prefer to memorialize my gratitude by capturing it in words that I write by hand and take the time to send. Add an invite to lunch (your treat), or send flowers. Think about it this way: your champion helped you in a meaningful way to pursue your dreams.

But you have so much to do as a business owner! How will you "find time" for this? You make time for what matters. If you're "too busy" to show your appreciation, then you send the message that your business is booming. Your champions will no longer go out of their way to help you. And they'll stop sending referrals. You're swamped. You don't even have the time to send a proper thank you. Or maybe, instead of thinking you're "too busy," your champions will interpret your response this way: she's ungrateful. And that's not true, right? You very much appreciate that they took the time to help you in a meaningful way to bring your business dreams to life. Show your champions your appreciation!

The Disneyland Effect

You have something to offer your champions, even at the earliest stage—before you launch your practice and gain your own lessons and practical pointers to share. When you're engaged in an endeavor that is true to you, people want to be in your presence. You light up from within. Share your enthusiasm. It's a gift you can give to others. Sometimes, people have experience, know-how, and valuable advice to share, but they have somehow lost sight of the why behind what they do. You can serve as their reminder. Reignite their spark by shining your light.

The learning curve is steep. You will need the most help at the onset of your business, when your enthusiasm is at its peak. Everything will be new and exciting. Allow the Disneyland Effect to take place. Think about why parents (and not just kids) love going to Disneyland. Experiencing it through their children's eyes brings magic back into their lives. There's magic in bringing one's dreams to life. Share the magic. Sprinkle it onto those whom you ask for help.

The Tenacity Ledger Technique

Inviting your champions to help you by making the CASA Ask is easy. You formulate a question that communicates how your champion can help you, and then you ask it. You've been asking questions since you started to toddle. The number one reason people fail to make the CASA Ask is not because the process itself is difficult; it's due to fear of rejection. To save themselves the pain of rejection, they foreclose the opportunity for a yes.

Why wouldn't your potential champion say yes? Get outside of yourself. How would you react to an enthusiastic individual reaching out to you in a personal way and wanting your help for something specific? If you'd cross your arms and say, "Why would I want to help you?" then I can see why you assume that others will reject you. You're projecting your own lack of generosity onto them.

But you're likely a generous person. You'd consider their ask and do what you could to help. You'd feel good about helping someone else in a meaningful way. Give your champions an opportunity to feel good about helping you to bring your business vision to life.

If you're hesitant to make the ask, consider that you have people in your life who want to help you, but they don't want to step on your toes. They're waiting for an invitation. A respectful ask is not intrusive; it's inclusive. You're welcoming them to take part in your bold endeavor.

Rethink rejection. Many entrepreneurs get in their own way, and this is a prime example: they see rejection as followed by a period, The End, instead of by a comma. Remove the emotional charge from a no, and then the way to move forward becomes simple: you ask someone else. Instead, an entrepreneur who gets in her own way takes rejection personally, sure that it's a reflection on her value and the worth of her vision.

Rejection is not about you. All that happened is that one person passed on the opportunity to help you to bring your vision to life. That's okay. You made the mistake of not preparing for a no. And you won't make it again.

Employ the Tenacity Ledger Technique. When I committed to launching my law practice, I bought a small notebook with an affirmation on the cover. It became my official "Tenacity Ledger" when I labeled it as such with a permanent marker. I developed a process: when I received a no, I'd write down my request and the steps I'd taken (including the ask that had led to a no). I'd brainstorm next steps, and write them in my ledger. I'd move on down the list until I found what I needed to move forward. With my plan for dealing with rejection in place, I started to reach out for help.

A year after I started it, I came across my Tenacity Ledger in a drawer. Either nobody had declined my invite, or, by the time that someone did, I had built such momentum that it hadn't fazed me enough to record. None were memorable. I racked my brain for a good example of a rejection to share with you and drew a blank.

The countless times I received practical pointers

and active efforts to help me better serve my clients made any rejection insignificant. I made a mindful, specific ask and showed my appreciation for whatever help my champions offered. My champions are marvelous. You, too, can have a community of champions in your life, a caring safety net underneath you as you launch your bold endeavor. Yes, you'll still have setbacks. But champions sure make it easier to rise and keep going.

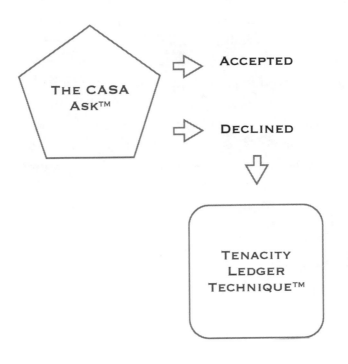

PART IV:

CLIENT RELATIONS

Let's review: You've unleashed your inner entrepreneur (if you have an entrepreneurial spirit), and built a business that is True to You. You've attracted your right-fit clients. What you say and do will determine whether they shift from potential clients to current clients, and then former satisfied clients.

13 THE SATISFIED-CLIENT ROADMAP

THE SATISFIED-CLIENT ROADMAP™

1. TAILOR YOUR SCHEDULE
2. CREATE THE RIGHT ENVIRONMENT
3. STRUCTURE YOUR INITIAL CONSULT
4. SET EXPECTATIONS
5. INVITE TO HIRE
6. MAKE MONEY TALK ROUTINE
7. PREPARE FOR A YES
8. COLLABORATE
9. CULTIVATE CLIENT SATISFACTION

Guidepost #1:
Tailor your schedule to
serve your right-fit clients.

Think about how your right-fit clients move through the process. Generally, my right-fit clients, first-timers, had no practical idea how to navigate the criminal justice system. Media portrayals are inaccurate. Left to their own devices, first-timers often damage their case prospects and go into a panic that the horrific scenarios played out on television will become their reality. Uncertainty terrifies people. Often, it causes either a head-in-the-sand approach, or brash action that has harsh consequences. My clients did not have the legal knowledge or practice experience to figure out what their entry into the system meant for their lives. The earlier I could enter the picture, educate them on the process, banish unfounded fears, and create a case plan, the better.

I mentioned earlier (in the Show Your Face section in Part II: Brand "You") that I showed up as an unconventional "face" in the criminal-defense directory circulated to jails. I knew that my right-fit clients first considered hiring a criminal-defense lawyer soon after their arrest. These calls most often came in between 10:00 p.m. and 2:00 a.m. on Thursday, Friday, and Saturday. Arrestees often called me as their first choice. Connecting with them at this early stage builds brand loyalty. Had I not answered my phone at those "ungodly" hours, I would have missed many opportunities to grow my practice.

Tailor your schedule to serve your right-fit clients. My current clients took priority. If I had court on a Friday morning for a current client, I would shut my phone off the prior Thursday night, even though I would miss potential-client calls. When I first launched my practice, I made the mistake of 24/7 lawyering, and discovered that I'm not a robot. Caffeine and willpower will only propel you so far for so long. Accommodate your potential and current clients, but remember that you're the goose that lays the golden eggs. Schedule in time for rest, fuel, sleep, and play to keep yourself in prime shape to produce.

Guidepost #2:
Create the right environment
for your right-fit clients.

My business decisions arose from imagining the process from my right-fit client's perspective. For instance, my right-fit client often did not sit in custody for the duration of his or her case. Because there was no set location (jail or court), I had to decide where to hold meetings. Many solo-practice lawyers skimp on the actual-office part to save on overhead. They have "virtual offices" that consist of a mailing address and then offer to make house calls, meet in the courthouse, or converse at a coffeehouse.

I considered the virtual-office option from my right-fit client's perspective. First-timers often have jobs, families—a whole life in which they are not considered a "criminal." Why would they opt to drag their mucky cases into their homes?

The courthouse presented other issues. It mortifies first-timers. They're nervous wrecks when they set foot in a courthouse. I didn't want to meet my potential clients in that frenzied state for an eleventh-hour discussion. (Quick—sign the representation agreement. Court starts in five minutes.) Instead, I wanted to converse in an environment conducive to clear thinking, fluid discussion, and careful decision-making, so that my clients would feel calm, clear, and certain when hiring me.

A first-timer wants a quiet, private setting in which to discuss this messy, scary situation. At a coffee shop, a kid at the next table might wail. The waitress might interrupt to ask if you want your coffee warmed. Maybe you're in a self-serve setting, and the lone guy sitting nearby seems awfully thoughtful. Potential Client is certain that he's listening to every word. Or, heaven forbid, someone that Potential Client knows walks through the door. Potential Client gets flustered and blurts out the big secret that she is charged with a criminal offense. And an awkward introduction ensues: "Please meet my attorney. Well, maybe my attorney. We haven't actually gotten around to discussing my case yet." The attorney chimes in. "Do you mind sitting over there so you can't hear us discuss her confidential case?"

I prevented the scenarios above, inspired by stories gleaned from other solo-practice lawyers, by meeting my potential clients in a professional, private setting. To decrease overhead, I shared office space with another solo-practice lawyer. I had access to two conference rooms where I welcomed my potential clients. In this professional, peaceful setting, the entire focus was on them.

Guidepost #3:
Structure your initial consult
around your potential client.

The top mistake attorneys make in counseling clients is that they make meetings be about themselves —not their clients! I was never late. And if my potential clients arrived early, I did everything possible to meet with them within minutes of their arrival. Other attorneys told me not to do this: I'd look desperate, too eager. It's better to be that oh-so-busy lawyer who schedules right down to the minute and appears not a moment sooner. That's baloney. Those same attorneys wailed and moaned that their right-fit clients were scarce.

My right-fit client (we'll call her Martha for this illustration) loved that she didn't have to wait and sit hostage to her fears about what this scary situation meant for her life. I could see that Martha had streamed questions through her mind, hoping not to forget a single one. You can imagine Martha's response when I entered reception with a warm, reassuring smile and a hand extended, locking my eyes on hers and waiting until she returned my smile to say, "I'm Rita Johansen. Thank you for taking the time to come to my office. Let's talk in my conference room." I set the tone for our meeting in these first moments. By holding out my hand and embracing hers, I sent the message I'd give her strength. I expressed my appreciation that she had come to my office. I allowed my reassuring smile to come all the way to my eyes.

And then I took charge. A criminal case is a scary concept to a neophyte. Martha needed to know that I was a capable, compassionate guide. Ushering her into my conference room, I positioned myself at the head of the table. Instead of starting the meeting by word-vomiting war stories and credentials onto her, I invited Martha to tell me what had happened, in her own words. In doing so, I ensured that she would be attentive and listening to what I had to say. And her recital allowed her to clear her mind. Otherwise, I would have put Martha in the position of mentally juggling her story, her fears, and her questions, all while trying valiantly to process what I had to say.

While paying attention to my potential client's story, I would look for body-language cues that signaled a reluctance to share: a trailing voice, gazing into the distance, biting the lip, darting eyes, covering the mouth, a heavy sigh, sagging shoulders. When I saw one of these cues, I would say something like this: "To help you, I have to know what happened. I'm interested in being your lawyer, not your judge." Another effective technique is to reach out your hand halfway to your potential client and rest it on the table. If your potential client wants a reassuring hand pat, he or she will bridge the gap. (Connection matters.) And then you say, "I know this is tough to talk about. All I ask is that you do your best. Okay?" You have a lot of leeway to press your potential clients to divulge information. The key is to do so with a gentle tone, kind eyes, and words that communicate your intention. Your potential clients need to know you aren't asking them to reveal themselves for criticism, judgment, blaming, or shaming.

By encouraging Martha to speak first, I had acknowledged her role as most valuable player on her legal team. I was the coach. My job was to get her ready for the game by explaining the rules in a language she understood (plain English, not legalese). After I explained the rules, I talked her through our game plan moving forward, integrating the facts she had shared.

Because I had created a receptive environment by first listening to what she had to say, Martha felt comfortable enough to ask me anything. Her questions illuminated what was most important to her to know: how her case would turn out, what did not make sense to her, and what she feared would happen. Martha did not require definitive answers to every question. But she wanted thoughtful responses that explained the rationale behind any perceived ambiguity.

Clients presume that you're competent to handle their cases. Don't ignore what they care about by "proving your competence" with war stories and credentials. Let your clients invite you to brag.

If they withhold that invite, resist. You cannot be an effective confidante if you're too busy puffing yourself up to listen. And it's in the confidante role that you find out the facts. If a client is comfortable and in storytelling mode, she's going to remember better than if you follow the Mr. Defender Model: set Martha further on edge with war stories, and then shoot questions at her like a firing squad. Mr. Defender gives her the legalese-laden version of how her case will work its way through the system. By the time he asks Martha if she has any questions, she's on mental overload and says no. He tells her not to worry her pretty little head. She's then dismissed.

My actions, words, and tone sent a different message to my potential client: this attorney accommodating, attentive, and appreciative. First impressions matter. Take care to set the right tone for your representation.

Guidepost #4: Set expectations.

Get clear on your potential client's expectations for representation. If you do not hear any expectations while listening to her story and her questions, then ask her what they are. You need to know them going in. If she has unrealistic expectations, then you need to know if she's open to education about the process. If you inform her that what she expects is not a reasonable outcome, and she is in denial, then by proceeding, you set yourself up to have an unsatisfied former client.

Sometimes, potential clients expect you to do things that you would never in a million years do. My first potential client, Tim, assured me that he could afford my services. I gently pressed. Tim meant that I could go to the ditch where he'd tossed a wad of cash upon his arrest, use it to cover his fee, and hold the rest until his release. His request tested my commitment to not judge. Feeling my jaw go slack, I made a conscious effort to close my mouth and give him a respectful response. He thought he had proposed a smart, creative solution. In a matter-of-fact tone, I told him it was against the law, my ethical duty as a lawyer, and my personal code of conduct. He looked surprised and told me that he'd met with an attorney earlier that day who was happy to do it. He'd expected unethical representation. I gathered my belongings to signal the interview was over and said, "Thank you for giving me the opportunity to discuss serving as your attorney. My law firm is not a good fit for you. I'll let you go so you can call another lawyer. Best of luck on your case." We shook hands. He thanked me for coming. We exchanged pleasant good-byes. However the interview ends, thank the potential client for the opportunity and wish them well. It's the right thing to do.

When your potential client asks you to engage in wrongdoing, it's a clear mismatch. However you tailor your style to your right-fit clients, you're ethical. This is nonnegotiable. I emphasize this because I have heard shocking comments from members of the GOBC about what they did "all the time." An example: Mr. Defender told me to give advice on how much marijuana someone could carry before moving from a misdemeanor to a felony.

"Isn't that counseling on how to commit wrongdoing?" I asked.

"I do it all the time. It's how I build trust with future potential drug clients. I also tell them to keep a stash of cash elsewhere for legal fees. That way, when they're charged down the road, they call me, and they have the cash to pay me. And I tell my prostitution clients to get the cops to feel them up. Cops aren't supposed to do that."

"Doesn't that violate the ethics rules?"

"You're new. You'll figure out your own style," he

said.

And so I emphasize this point: the co-conspirator approach to client counseling is not a stylistic difference. It's outright wrong.

Only if your potential client is a right fit for your firm should you move onto Guidepost 5 and invite him or her to hire you. Otherwise, thank your potential client for the opportunity and end the meeting.

Guidepost #5:
Invite your potential right-fit client to hire you.

When your goal is to close the deal, you build your sales pitch up to the crescendo. And then you give your potential client the one-two punch for the knockout. You close the deal and pump your fist in victory. If you fail to knock out your potential client, then you hang your head in shame and throw your boxing gloves against the wall, convinced you were robbed.

But when your intention is to discover whether you and your potential client are a good fit for each other, you judge victory by whether you did your best at what you have control over: how well you listened for clues about your potential client's expectations and communicated your ability to live up to these expectations. You respect your potential client's sovereignty over her own life. She, not you, is best suited to make the decision whether you're a good fit as her

lawyer. You cannot know all that goes into her deci-
sion within the time allotted for the initial meeting.
She has her reasons, and they're valid.

After I determined that Martha was a right fit for
my firm, I reviewed the terms of my representation
agreement. And then I segued into extending the in-
vite to become my client. "I've enjoyed getting to
know you today, Martha. I've explained the process—
your role in it and mine. We've talked about what you
can expect from me moving forward. Have I done a
good job of explaining what will happen in your
case?"

"Yes. You've been really helpful in answering my
questions."

"Thank you, Martha. I keep my clients informed
every step of the way. As I said before, you're the
most important person on your legal team. It's your
case, and your life. I'm here to help you meet your
expectations for your case. You understand that I
cannot guarantee an outcome, but I will work hard
for you."

"Oh, yeah, what did you call your style again?"

I grinned and said, "Respectfully tenacious. Would
you like me to use my respectfully tenacious style to
represent you, Martha?"

She laughed and asked, "Do you have a pen?"

Guidepost #6: Make money talk routine.

By the time I transitioned into reviewing the representation agreement, Martha had experienced a meaningful sample of how I represented my clients. And then I didn't make money talk awkward, as some attorneys do by clearing their throats and pulling at their collars. Or worse—they apologize for their fees! If you think that your fee requires an apology, then slash it. If, instead, you charge a reasonable fee in line with the effort you expend and expertise you use to represent your clients, announce it in a matter-of-fact tone. I presented my fee in the same, no-nonsense way I had reviewed the other points in the representation agreement. Martha could afford my fee.

Avoid payment plans (like the plague, if you're in criminal defense, unless you're willing to accept the first payment as your entire fee.) Your unqualified client will have myriad excuses for not making subsequent payments. You'll have no way to know whether they're true. But you'd look like a real jerk for insisting you get your full fee when they frame the situation as paying you or the hospital for an emergency medical procedure, or the mechanic for car repair so they can get to work. You'll hear everything that they could be doing with their hard-earned money instead of paying their lawyer. Clients assume that lawyers live in sandstone castles high up in the hills. They don't care about your bills, but you do.

If you learn this lesson the hard way, that's okay. You'd be hard-pressed to find a nice professional who hasn't fallen for the old I'm-going-to-pay-you-later-I-pinky-swear routine. The real jerks have no problem saying sayonara. It's as easy to them as wiping the mud off their shiny shoes.

In the unqualified potential client's defense, she may be entirely sincere about paying you in the microscopic moment. And then she telescopes out of it into her daily routine. Her medical statement comes in. The rent or mortgage is due. Her car stalls. And you are way over yonder in your grand castle. If you find yourself in this situation, don't beat yourself up. Being kind is wonderful, but you need to work on strengthening your spine to run a private practice, not a legal charity. It's entirely within your control to never be in this sticky situation again.

I didn't shake down a potential client by insisting that she could afford my fee. She had a much better handle on her financial situation than I did. If she told me she could not afford my fee, I thanked her for considering me as her lawyer, and wished her all the best.

Clients are street savvy. They won't pay your full fee if they think you'll give them a discount. I didn't negotiate my price. That would set my client up for wondering if I had swindled her. Had he held out, could he have gotten a better deal? I worked toward a transparent, trusting relationship and didn't want to torpedo my own efforts. Don't play games with the fee: calculate, charge—and commit.

You must decide whether you want to have a policy for handling discounted cases, instead of just releasing every unqualified right-fit client. If you elect the former route, then have a policy in place. Otherwise, you set yourself up to fail when faced with the inevitable potential client's financial-straits story that tugs at your heartstrings. I had a "low-fee" policy (instead of a for-free, pro bono policy), under which I allowed one discounted case on my roster at a time.

When I had the low-fee client slot open, I would invite a financially unqualified right-fit client to take advantage of my policy: "As I said, Janice, for your particular legal situation, my regular fee would be $2,495. I feel for your financial situation, and I really want to help you. Here's what I'm able to do. My office policy is to take on one discounted case at a time. I do not currently have one on my roster. I would be happy to help you, Janice, for $995. This is the very best that I can do." I was upfront about my policy, because my low-fee clients needed to understand that they were exceptions. Otherwise, they might have misled referrals by telling them something like this: "She charges a third of what the other guys charge!"

Your low-fee clients may send you qualified referrals. More likely, they will send you others like themselves seeking to take advantage of your policy. And so, when you are deciding whether to have this policy, I'd suggest not considering it as a way to grow your business. Much more effective strategies exist. My low-fee policy was simply the way I could offer more affordable legal representation to my community without bankrupting my private practice.

I caution you against accepting low-fee *misfit* clients. My low-fee policy applied to potential clients who fit my firm but could not pay my full fee. I still found it rewarding to serve my low-fee clients, and my low-fee clients were still possible (although unlikely) sources for qualified referrals. In contrast, the "low-fee" misfit client is a drain, and a dead end.

Guidepost #7: Prepare for a yes.

Client counseling is not a scientific process. Nor is it the type of art where you grab random tools and start doodling. Following the guideposts described above and being prepared to move forward contributed to my perfect closure rate for qualified right-fit clients. If you're not prepared to move forward with confidence, why would your potential client hire you? Have any paperwork ready that you will need to represent your client. And have a pen handy. Nothing says you're unprepared for a yes like failing to have a pen to offer your potential client when it's time to sign the representation agreement.

For instance, for a DUI case, I'd print out the

chapters to study for the DUI driving test and an information packet on the Ignition Interlock Device Program. I'd slide these materials into a folder and include my business card, if she seemed like a good fit. I would give her this folder before reviewing the terms of my representation agreement. It added credibility to my statement that I wanted to help her. And it sent the message that I would hit the ground running.

If she did not seem like a good fit, I would not send mixed signals by giving her materials with my firm name on them, to forestall a later call in which I would have to spend time on an avoidable, redundant conversation. Part ways on good terms, and do not give a non-right-fit client anything that she could interpret as a lifeline to your firm.

Guidepost #8: Collaborate with your clients.

Instead of benching my clients as passive spectators in the Defender Showcase, I encouraged my clients to get in the game. In the case of a DUI, I listed the next steps for my client to take: the forms to complete and where to send them, appointments to set up, proofs that would be helpful— of employment, of community service. I knew that first-timers do better if they have something tangible to accomplish. Left idle, they will wring their hands and concoct worst-case scenarios.

Sometimes when my clients called, it wasn't for *something*, it was for *connection*, like Abigail. It was the night before her first hearing, and Abigail was nervous. She wanted to talk to me—her confidante, her advisor. What would you say in this situation? "I have everything under control. Stop worrying." *Click*. No, I didn't say that. I said, "What you're feeling, Abigail, is perfectly understandable. Your case matters to you, and to me. It's okay to be nervous about it. Would it help to walk through your part again?"

She sighed in relief and said, "Yes."

I talked her through it from the perspective of a neophyte to the justice system. "You'll get to the courthouse half an hour early. Go through security. Right after security there will be screens. Find your name and courtroom number. I'll sit on a bench across from it and wait for you. All you have to do tomorrow is get through security, and I'll be right there waiting for you. How does that sound?"

"Good. I can do that."

"Absolutely. I'm here for you, Abigail. Call me if you need me."

Did my client find this patronizing? No—it's helpful information when you've never been to court and you fear it will be the place where your whole life might be torpedoed. All you have to do is show up, find your courtroom, and your attorney will be there for you. I was a professional with special skills and knowledge, willing and able to connect with my clients on a human level. The danger of being seen by your clients as impenetrable, lofty, and inaccessible is that they may use you as a dartboard, fail to give you the benefit of the doubt, and feel alone and isolated throughout the process—even though you show up for them at court and speak fluent legalese.

By collaborating with my clients, I built Credibility Capital. I told them that I'd be available, and then I answered my phone; I painted a picture of what would happen in court, and it came to life.

Every time that you tell your client what will happen and it comes true, you build credibility. When you have Credibility Capital to cash in, it's much easier to convince the MVP of the legal team to participate. She trusts that you make good calls and that you're invested in getting her home. For most professionals, "getting her home" is a metaphor for meeting your client's expectations for her case. But for professionals like me, who represent first-timers to the criminal justice system, this is also a reflection of their clients' greatest hope: to literally go home (not to jail or prison).

At her second hearing, Abigail said, "I thought about calling you last night, but then I thought, Rita has this, and I calmed down. I slept surprisingly well last night. I'm really glad you're my lawyer." When you take the time to connect and collaborate, you receive affirmations like this one from your clients.

When you receive an affirmation, it is a prime opportunity to reciprocate. I said, "Thank you for your kind words, Abigail. You're a wonderful client. It matters that you voluntarily started treatment. I appreciate that you're doing all that you can for your case." You point to a specific way that your client has shown up for herself. People respond well to positive reinforcement. My first- time clients beat themselves up enough about landing in the criminal justice system; I kept them focused on what they could do to move forward and then affirmed them for doing it. Maybe they started classes toward a postsecondary degree. Maybe they were diligent in getting proof of employment from their employer. Notice and appreciate your clients' efforts to do their best in their cases.

Guidepost #9: Cultivate client satisfaction.

Client satisfaction is based on how the attorney's representation lived up to or fell short of the client's expectations. In other words, it is client driven. You must make her aware of the stellar work that you did behind the scenes to meet her expectations. Don't leave her satisfaction to chance by failing to find out her expectations at the get-go. And check in along the way. Your client will like that you care enough to inquire.

I asked Martha, "How do you feel about how your case is going? Is it meeting your expectations so far?"

"Yes," Martha said. "It's just how you said it would

be."

A satisfied client is not created only at the instant the case is resolved. Put in the work upfront. Explain and demystify the process. Guide and engage your client. Communicate to your client that something meaningful has happened on her case. Doing the work upfront means that you don't have to backtrack. It's much harder to cultivate satisfaction after your client has felt lost, abandoned, or confused. Plant satisfaction seeds early, when the ground is fertile, and water them along the way. Don't wait until the ground is dry and cracked.

When the case is over, have a debrief session. Talk about how the case met the client's expectations. Send a letter that captures in writing the case resolution and state that this concludes your representation. Copy and include documents for their file about the resolution. Express your genuine sentiments about how wonderful it was to work with her. And invite her to take a client- satisfaction survey. Explain that you strive to represent each client with excellence, and you'd appreciate any feedback they may have about your representation.

When you receive the survey back, send a handwritten thank-you card. That card presents another opportunity to show your appreciation to your former client for taking the time to help you to have a stellar law practice. You note that you appreciate their kind words, and reciprocate by including your own: *I ad-*

mired your positive attitude in the midst of a tough situation. Or, I'm delighted to hear that you're enrolled in nursing school. You'll make a caring and attentive nurse.

The client survey also gives your former client a chance to practice forming meaningful feedback about you as her lawyer. She'll be ready to answer this questions: Do you know a good lawyer?

If you do not pay attention to feedback during representation or inquire about it if not volunteered, then you have set yourself up for later damage control. The worst time to be told that you fell short in some way is after the case is over, when it's too late to do anything about it. Take responsibility for doing everything that is within your power to cultivate a satisfied former client. Be proactive: set expectations and live up to them. Inquire periodically to see if your client is satisfied with how you're doing on her case. That inquiry does not reflect a lack of confidence, it reflects reality: you're not a mind reader. Instead of guessing about satisfaction level, ask your client. Then, by the time you ask for a formal response to the question of how you did, you'll already know that you hit a home run.

And when that great event happens, what do you do next? You look around to see if there were witnesses. You want everyone to know about this feat. When people ask you what's new, bring it up. You hit one over the fence! Obtain permission from your client to share it. Include a box on the survey that your former client can check to give you permission to use their comments in your law- firm promotions. Feature these testimonials on your online presence. Use them in oral communications about your firm, not just in print. Get creative. Tell others who ask you for an update on your business: "It's going great! I just closed another case, and my former client called me a godsend! It's so rewarding to have that kind of feedback. I sure love what I do!"

14 MY MISFIT-CLIENT STORY

Gary's attorney had been removed from his case due to a conflict of interest. According to his prior lawyer, Gary had refused to consider a negotiated outcome and was tracked for trial. A regular in the justice system, seasoned and cynical, Gary was a misfit for my firm. But out of a misplaced empathy, I invited Gary to hire me, and at a discounted rate. He did.

Taking Gary on as a client had some big negative consequences. The opportunity costs went beyond time invested in Gary's case that I could have spent on attracting potential right-fit clients. Because like associates with like, after Gary sang my praises around the jailhouse, I received calls from potential misfit clients and spent my most precious resources (time and energy) on fielding these calls, amicably turning down each one. I think that this is the worst part of handling a case for a misfit client: you're not rewarded for doing a great job—no intrinsic glow, no word-of-mouth referrals for right-fit clients.

Allow me to elaborate. The costs that had dollar figures attached meant less to me than the emotional toll. I cared far more about Gary's case than he did. He had accepted that someday his lifestyle would garner him a long prison sentence. It was only a matter of time. He was resigned to his "fate." In me, he'd found someone who wanted to get to know him: what he wanted out of his case, and his life. His dull eyes started to come alive. After months of insisting to his prior lawyer that he had no interest in negotiating a plea deal, Gary revealed to me what he really wanted: a contact visit with his toddler son. He wanted to hug and kiss his boy before breaking the news face to face that Daddy was going to prison. In the end, he broke many hearts: his mom's, his girlfriend's, his son's, mine, and his own.

Many factors contributed to this young man's presence in the criminal justice system. By the time I entered the picture, tsunami waves were ready to crash over his head. They'd been building for a long time. I tried to save Gary from drowning. By caring enough to help him get what mattered most in his case, I think I accomplished this goal. Mr. Defender, Gary's prior lawyer, had no idea that Gary even had a son. Mr. Defender may have assumed that what mattered most to Gary was less prison time. But all Gary wanted was to hold his son before his transfer from jail to prison, and this was a criminal case (and life) decision that was his to make.

Client relations are complex when you care: when your clients aren't cardboard cutouts of each other, when you make them three-dimensional by discovering their expectations and aspirations. I did deep soul-searching after Gary's case. I could impact the lives of those entrenched in the system by creating a lawyer-client relationship in which they felt safe enough to admit what really mattered, instead of hiding behind a tough-guy front—Gary's persona when I first met him. After I had created a safe environment, the tough guy had fallen away, and he had become a frightened young man, not yet twenty, resigned to a bleak cycle. What ray of light did he have in his life? His child.

The Gary Case illustrates this reality about client work: a professional-services firm involves a person serving another person. The professional who ignores her client's emotions is not a full- service provider. When Gary started to cry, I didn't just toss him a tissue and bolt, assuring him that I'd return when he got himself under control so we could go back to the business of discussing his case. Gary had been at the brink of a breakthrough. He was about to reveal what he wanted most from the prosecutor. Had I abandoned him when he showed vulnerability, he might have shut down again. He'd have received the message that that his hopes had no place in his case. These moments give us professional-service providers an opportunity to connect with our clients on a human level. Both a victim of society and its criminal outcast, Gary had traveled a life path I can only imagine. But I know what it is to love a child.

You have limited time and energy. And so you have to make tough choices about where to focus them. A private defender has an endless supply of potential clients like Gary. By accepting them all, I would have ripped apart my ship and served no one. Decisions that cause a big drain on your firm (and on you) happen. Don't bury your head and beat yourself up. See them instead as opportunities to rise, look around, and figure out the lessons.

The Gary Case focused my vision for my right-fit client: the first-timer who didn't think of himself or herself as a "criminal," who wanted to do what it took to move into a better chapter that didn't include the criminal justice system. It's an aspiration; I couldn't make my clients break free from their quicksand. But I could help them to do their work. To serve those like Gary (neck deep in the system) whom I might be able to tug up for a breath of fresh air before they went under did not fit my firm.

The more information I had, the better decisions I made. How many misfit clients did I accept? One: Gary. You may make a different decision, and accept misfit clients. Given unlimited resources (time, energy, and funds), I would have happily accepted as a client every Gary who called my firm. I had been ready (and, frankly, excited) to duke it out at trial. But I stayed focused on Gary.

As the prosecutor and I called each other to discuss trial logistics and propose offers during the weekend leading up to the trial date, the prosecutor pressed me, "Is this really going to go? I'm sacrificing my weekend for this." And this is when I hear stories about how other defenders throw their clients under the bus with this type of response: "I'll talk my client into a deal. Take it easy." Or, "You bet this is going to trial. Buckle up." Either response would have robbed Gary of the decision that's rightfully his to make.

I understood the prosecutor's perspective. Trial work is the most time-intensive, mentally taxing part of criminal-law practice. It is also how we make a criminal defendant's right to trial meaningful. My client had rejected the state's offer, and at that point Gary was exercising his right to go to trial. Every time the prosecutor inquired, "Is this really going to go?" I said something like this: "My client would consider another offer. He is aware of when your current offer expires, and has decided not to accept it at this time. I'm happy to go over again what he's willing to accept." The prosecutor would reply, "I can't give your client what he's asking for." And I'd say, "Then yes, I'm prepared to go to trial for my client. And no, we're not wasting your time. You know as well as I do that this is my client's call to make, not mine."

Representing criminal-defense clients requires the defender to pursue two paths to resolution at the same time: a litigated or a negotiated resolution. Even as you prepare witnesses, review evidence, plan examinations (and the trial tasks go on and on), you keep the communication channels to the state wide open to secure the best possible offer for your client. The decision to go through with trial, or to accept a plea, rests with the client. And the client has more time than you might think to decide. To simplify, think of it as running right up until the jury sits to hear the case. The defender that shuts down negotiations before that moment (to focus on the upcoming flashy defender showcase) is not doing everything in his power to serve his client. Ultimately, I secured (through respectfully tenacious negotiations) an offer that included what Gary wanted most from his case. Gary decided to accept it.

Working with Gary was rewarding. But I had finite time, energy, and funds. I ran a business using an unconventional model that had attracted clients like crazy. Because I had attracted more potential clients than I could accommodate, I had to figure out whom I would accept on my case roster. After Gary, I created a placeholder among my qualified right-fit clients and made a modification to my firm's "low-fee" policy: This slot was reserved for an unqualified *right-fit* client, who fit my firm in every other way but could not afford my fee. Consider my misfit-client story when you encounter a Gary of your own. If you choose to accept misfit clients, I caution you to do so after careful consideration (and once in a blue moon).

MISFIT CLIENT (MC)
CHALLENGE QUESTIONS:

+ WHY DID YOU ACCEPT MC?
+ WHAT MADE MC A POOR FIT FOR YOUR FIRM?
+ WHAT DID YOU GIVE UP TO SERVE MC?
+ WHAT WAS MISSING?
+ WHAT DID YOU DO RIGHT?
+ WHAT DOES THIS EXPERIENCE ADD TO YOUR VISION FOR YOUR RIGHT-FIT CLIENT?

15 DOCUMENT YOUR DILIGENCE

Many professionals are diligent, but stumble on this step: Document your diligence. Be ready to show what you did for your clients. I'd regularly call, email, and send snail mail to my clients to let them know what I was doing behind the scenes, and to show them that I cared. Before calling a client, I would prepare a checklist in advance and take time after each call to add any other important information that I had relayed before putting the legal pad back in the case file. I'd print off emails, copy sent mail, and file these client communications. I worked hard for them. And, because of my frequent client communications, my clients knew it.

My diligence paid off when unforeseen circumstances affected my law practice in a big way. Placed on medical leave, I had to withdraw from my active cases. And then I discovered there is a downside to building strong connections with my clients. We were a team, and their coach was leaving mid-season. They did not want any other coach—any other attorney to handle their cases. But they had to go into the criminal-defense seascape and find a new one; the ethics rules barred me from cherry- picking new attorneys for them.

I followed my procedure for closing a case file. For

example, I gave Peter an accounting letter detailing my work, and I enclosed a copy of his representation agreement and a check for the portion of the fee I had not yet earned, along with an additional amount as a good-faith refund. Peter went to find a new criminal-defense attorney and hired Mr. Defender. According to Peter, Mr. Defender sent him to tell me to return more money or he'd report me to the ethics committee and bar associations. Seeking a second opinion, I called an attorney who had served as an ethics investigator, who seconded my take on the situation: Mr. Defender was trying to bully me (via my former client) into transferring money from my pocket to his.

Riled up by Mr. Defender, Peter filed a complaint with the ethics committee. I found this out two weeks later, when I received a letter from the Office of Lawyers Professional Responsibility. Without any investigation, the Office dismissed my former client's complaint. Citing my representation agreement, the accounting letter, and the good-faith refund as support, the Office determined that discipline was not warranted. (My former client had kindly included these exhibits with his complaint.) I had to do no further work to prove I'd acted ethically. I'd put the work in along the way—preparing a clear representation agreement, documenting my diligence, accounting for my work and my fee, and timely return of the portion of the fee I hadn't yet earned. I had even gone above and beyond, because it felt right, and returned extra money as a good-faith refund, because my medical leave had inconvenienced Peter. He'd had to go out and find other counsel. (Peter hired alternate counsel the very day I withdrew with no adverse impact on his case prospects.)

Sometimes, the unforeseen happens. When it does, stand up for the hard work that you've done thus far in your former client's case. Charge a reasonable amount for your services. Return any overage, and an additional amount as a good-faith refund if that's true to you. Realize those gestures will likely still not satisfy your former client, because you have not met his expectations. That's okay. Accept that you cannot satisfy every former client on all points in every situation. In Peter's case, my medical leave barred me from meeting his expectations.

People-pleasing cannot be your standard of doing business. You must set expectations, work hard to meet them, and make amends to the best of your ability if the unforeseen happens and you fall short. Some concerns override client satisfaction, such as the attorney's health.

PART V: TEND TO YOU

16 TIME FOR SELF

As an entrepreneur, there's a time to turn on the three D's (Drive, Discipline, and Determination), and a time to hit pause. This will look different depending on your practice area. For me, it meant a willingness to turn off my phone and accept that I'd miss overnight jail calls. Otherwise (and I made this mistake many times), I'd wake at 2:00 a.m. to field a jail call and still find myself in my office by 7:00 a.m. for a twelve-hour day. I loved my practice. But I learned the hard way that I'm not a robot.

There is another pragmatic reason to hit pause. Though you are on a mental break, your subconscious will continue to work. Expect inspiration to strike in unexpected places. A creative resolution came to me while I sat watching sailboats bob on Lake Calhoun; when I returned to my office, my client approved this proposed resolution. Later on, the prosecutor accepted it.

Ideas for what to do when you hit pause on your practice:

Meditation. Quiet your mind. If your mind chatters, use a mantra. Persevere. With practice, you'll learn to quiet your thoughts. When I started to meditate, all I could think about was the mile-long to-do list I could be tackling instead of wasting my time trying to meditate. But I kept at it. I carved out twenty minutes to sit still and wait for the swirling debris (my chatterbox mind) to settle into stillness. Meditation allowed me to connect with my core. My instincts grew stronger to better guide my true-to-me practice.

Exercise. Practice yoga. And no, you don't have to be pretzel-flexible. Jog in the crisp morning hours to the soothing sounds of footfalls and birdsong. Take work at a slower pace. You don't even have to wait until you leave your office and change into athletic gear. Lock the door, take off your suit coat, turn on a song that gets your blood pumping, and dance. I kayak, hike, cross-country ski, and practice therapeutic yoga.

Hobbies. Buy a book from your reading list. Treat yourself to a couple chapters over tea or coffee. Revive rusty hobbies, or embrace a new one. I invent recipes, scrapbook, and go on treasure hunts to capture beauty with my camera.

Connection. Turn off your electronics and connect in person. Share your stories with those who care about you and your endeavors. And listen. I call this cathartic connection. You get to speak to what resides in your heart and hear what resides in the hearts of others. Uplift each other.

17 FREE YOUR SELF

I will leave you with one last tale, and it is a cautionary one. It illustrates the danger of staying at the helm of your ship—*whatever* happens, no matter what. I discovered my threshold for "whatever." Many entrepreneurs don't reach this end of the spectrum: unfettered determination to make their business work no matter what, including self-sacrifice. I did. It snuck up on me; I was like a live lobster dipped in water that's heated until the unsuspecting crustacean is cooked.

As I showed up for my right-fit clients, the captain's wheel firmly in hand, the water became a bit choppier, but not enough to quell my delight at representing my right-fit clients. Illness was entering my life slowly. And I was too stubborn to acknowledge it. The demands of law practice explained away the eleven pounds that vanished from my petite frame, and the exhaustion.

Then fatigue grew more insistent, and refused to be ignored any longer. I caved, admitting I needed to acknowledge this unwelcome entrant into my life and see a doctor. My primary care physician ordered generic blood work.

"Hello, Rita. It's Dr. Abel. I'm calling to tell you that you have leukopenia." "Oh, my God, leukemia?"

"No, no, I'm not saying that."

"Well, what are you saying?"

"I'm saying you have leuk-o-pe-nia."

"I'm saying I don't know what that is."

"Oh, well, it means your white blood cell count is low—four-point-two when it should be four-point-five."

"I don't know how to judge these numbers, Doctor. What does that mean? What now?" "You could see a hematologist if you wanted to be thorough. The cause could be a virus. It's possible it could be something more serious." "Do you think I need to see a hematologist?"

"I'd be comfortable monitoring your progress and retesting your blood if you continue to have symptoms."

"Yeah, I'm comfortable with that too."

"Then I won't place a hematology referral at this time."

"Ok. Thanks, Doctor Abel."

"You're welcome. Take care."

Denial kept me from asking about something more serious.

Over the following months, Denial visited me regularly at my criminal-defense firm. I'd started to spend my days alternating between calm, cool, and collected (sheer confidence) and panic attacks. I dismissed these signs. *I know why you are having panic attacks*, Denial insisted. *It is just the price you pay for launching a law practice as a new lawyer.* I cut through the exhaustion with more espresso, the panic with willpower. I wouldn't let them stop me.

Pop-Tart Rita disappeared. I forgot what it felt like to be her. In my weakened state, if she'd burst into my bedroom where I lay in the fetal position and put her chipper face near mine, commanding me with "Out of bed, Sleepyhead," I would've had no energy to either smack the smile off her face or smother her with my pillow—though the desire to do both. I didn't recognize the flattened, defeated, irritable person I became during an attack.

Dr. Abel again checked my blood, and no longer waffled. I needed to see a hematologist—and soon. *You'll see a specialty white coat and return to business as usual,* Denial reassured me.

Still at the helm of my ship, I continued to spend my most precious resources (energy and time) on serving my clients. They needed my ship to stay afloat —an emotionally intelligent law firm, a safe haven in a female-unfriendly practice sea.

When I cruised into the medical building, I expected a Minnesota Hematology sign. The suite number was right; the sign must be wrong: Minnesota Oncology. Eager to leave, I darted to the receptionist. "Excuse me, I'm here for hematology, not oncology. Where should I check in?"

"Right here. We don't do just cancer here."

I passed her my insurance cards, filled out forms, and sat to wait. *Instead of cancer, they think I have . . . something else, but just as bad??* Denial had no reply now.

A nurse's aide led me to the exam room, took my vitals, and left me with no answers in exchange. I was ready to bolt. And then the hematologist walked in. I liked her gentle smile and lilting accent; I'd dislike her if c-a-n-c-e-r came out of her mouth, unless she prefaced it with "absolutely not," or "you don't have."

She listened to my symptoms.

I eased back and set down the coffee mug I'd been clutching in an iron fist, unarmed for the blow she delivered.

"I disagree with your primary," she said. "Your symptoms aren't consistent with a leukemia—or any lymphoma-type blood disorder. They are more consistent with an autoimmune disorder, such as systemic lupus." She then ordered more blood work.

A nurse broke the news later that day: "Mrs. Johansen, you don't have systemic lupus."

Hooray! Right? Having supplied seventeen vials of my precious lifeblood expecting a firm conclusion, I had mixed feelings. The hematologist then suggested that I see *more* specialists: a rheumatologist, a gastroenterologist, a neurologist, a cardiologist, or an infectious-disease doctor. I imagined the Wheel of Fortune, each specialty in a slot, and spinning it—hoping to hit the jackpot, to land on the specialist who'd find the cause of my rapid decline and reverse it. But first, I had to go back to where I had begun: Dr. Abel's office. When she gave the Wheel of Specialists a spin, it landed on gastroenterology.

The gastroenterologist wanted samples, and I provided them. The results: normal.

"Mrs. Johansen, your doctor would like you to schedule an exploratory endoscopy and colonoscopy," a nurse said.

The exploratory part meant that the gastroenterologist had no suspect. It was a last-ditch effort to find something in her area that would explain some symptoms, and leave the rest to another specialty visit: the migraines, the panic attacks, the brain fog, the relentless fatigue—what I most wanted explained.

"Well, that sounds invasive," I said. "No. The doctor didn't say what she's looking for. I'm not comfortable with a fishing expedition on the off-chance we catch something."

"Mrs. Johansen, the doctor ordered it. You must schedule it." The nurse sounded shocked. A patient had refused to follow a doctor's order. She's the *doctor*; I was merely the *patient*. I had to let her poke and prod where the sun didn't shine, right?

"Well, it's my throat and my rear. They're not open for viewing. Thank you very much. Enjoy your weekend."

Dr. Abel hadn't hit the jackpot on the second try.

Returning to my primary doctor, I refused to let her spin the Wheel of Specialists again. I requested a referral to Mayo Medical Center, convinced I needed a team of specialists that talked to each other.

My appointment date loomed in the distance. I

had my suit on and my lawyer hat in place, and was in court standing for a client. While my handcuffed client watched, I lost consciousness and collapsed. The bailiff caught me before I could crack my head on the swinging solid oak divider. I went to the ER for four hours. After fast-tracking me into my own private ER suite, the ER doctor told me he thought it was something serious: a blood clot in my lung. Wearied from my months-long stay in the land of limbo, I yearned for certainty and readied myself to be wheeled into an operating room that evening.

The ER doctor delivered the results. "The good news is that everything came back negative. The bad news is that we can't explain your collapse. Your blood pressure could plummet again without warning. There's nothing you can do to prevent it. See a cardiologist within forty-eight hours." He released me back into my old indeterminate state.

The morning after my collapse, I returned to my office. My body felt like I'd put it through an old-fashioned, hand-cranked wringer and hung it on a wash line where it had been whipped by a strong wind. My inner champion said, *Give it all up.* But I had too far to travel yet to understand this instruction; I couldn't listen to hopelessness whispering in my ear. I'd been living my vision! How could I give it up?

And so I powered through with caffeine and willpower. I was typing a memorandum when the next episode descended. My thoughts hazed in my hijacked mind. Familiar with the progression, my limbs becoming heavy and weak, I walked over to my office's main door, knowing I had only minutes before my limbs would become too clunky to move. I flipped the lock. I flipped the lock. Nobody had ever been able to quell my attacks. And so I decided not to bother anyone. I'd ride it out, as I had all the others. And I'd do it alone.

Stumbling and then crawling, I made it to my cluttered storage area, to the makeshift cardboard mat I'd stashed for myself in the corner, and curled in the age-old position. It gave only small comfort. Hands clutched to my chest, I felt my heart threaten to burst free from its cage. An ice pick dug deep into my murky mind.

So this is dying. Thank God for some privacy to do it. I'd like to tell you I had a profound inner soliloquy to usher my spirit out of my body. The truth is that it was only a disjointed stream of snippets. *Guess I'll never use that new scanner. I wonder who'll get it when I go. I could crawl to my phone and call nine-one-one. What's the point? The ER had their crack at it. I'll end up back here again anyway. Probably tomorrow. I guess the dying don't care where they're taken. Here's as good a final resting place as any other.* I visualized an hourglass funneling sand into a cone and prepared for the last grain to fall.

When the attack eased back into the ethers as nonsensically as it had descended, my spirit remained in my body.

And I got up off the floor. I straightened my lapels, brushed off my pants, and thought I might use that scanner after all. And then I returned to my chair to finish my client's memorandum.

The days passed.

Chained to the wheel of my ship, I had steered through the latest storm. I held Hope to my chest, and squeezed her tightly. At the next appointment, a specialist would hit the jackpot, and then prescribe the Magic Pill that would return me to wellness. The rough seas would become a distant memory. I'd hand-selected an associate to meet the growing demand for my law firm's services. She's expressed her enthusiasm. And I'd told her that we'd have to wait until this medical storm passed.

Optimistic, I saw the cardiologist. He focused on my youth and upcoming Mayo Clinic appointment.

"Eat more salt," he said.

"I've disgusted my husband with how much salt I dump on my food. It's not humanly possible for me to consume more, short of salting my water."

"That's a fine idea. And drink more coffee. Caffeine won't hurt you."

"But I'm up to two large lattes a day. What about my chest pain? My heart palpitations?"

"Let's start conservatively. Increase your salt and caffeine. I've ordered an echocardiogram. I'd like you to return after the salt has had time to take effect."

"How long will that take?"

"One to two weeks."

"So you want to follow up in two weeks?"

"I was thinking more like five weeks. I mean six." But then he changed course entirely. "There's no need to follow up after Mayo," he said. After scrubbing his hands at the sink, ridding himself of any trace of me, he left the exam room.

Still hopeful, I thought that he'd stumbled upon the jackpot with the echocardiogram. He hadn't; I was normal. Normal. Normal. If this was how normal people felt, then I refused to remain in their ranks, or surrender to this thing hijacking my system. Stubborn as a mule, I trudged along, and made it to my long-anticipated finish line: the Mayo Clinic.

For two days, Mayo tested me, imaged my organs, and examined my fluids. I hit three different Divisions: Internal Medicine, Neuropathology, and Cardiology. My travels around the complex ended in the office of a hyper-specialized cardiologist.

"Your tests have come back in the normal range. Your heart is functioning properly. I've seen no structural defects. We see this all the time with women your size. You were born this way. You're too petite to stabilize your blood pressure."

"With all due respect, Doctor, that doesn't make sense. I wasn't born this way. For twenty-five years, I was extremely healthy and energetic with occasional bouts of lightheadedness—nothing like in the last year. So I'm suddenly too petite? I've been this size since I was thirteen. For twelve years, my blood pressure was ideal."

He looked at me like a father looks at a child about to throw a tantrum. "Rita, we didn't find anything else wrong with you. You're just too petite to support a normal blood pressure. I'm going to give you a prescription for a vasoconstrictor. It'll constrict your blood vessels to elevate your blood pressure. We'll start you on the smallest dose."

"Is that drug dangerous?"

"You'll need to be vigilant about following the instructions. Read the accompanying information closely. Make sure you don't lie down within four hours of taking this medication. You'd be at risk of hypertensive stroke."

"What'll I do if I get one of my attacks and have to lie down?"

"This medication will prevent an attack. It'll stabilize your blood pressure."

"How long will it take to have an effect? Days?"

"No, hours. It acts quickly to constrict the blood vessels. We'll know within the first twenty-four hours if it's working."

I can't isn't in a Mayo doctor's capacity to say aloud. It hadn't been in mine, either, until attacks had flattened me. Perfectionists abhor this phrase. So the Mayo doctor manufactured an answer that defied my expertise as a trained lawyer: logic.

I got what I'd wanted: the diagnosis and a Mayo

Magic Pill. Suddenly Too Petite: its stench spread in my mind to the other women I knew had been pushed out the door with this diagnosis and a Magic Pill. The drug sounded dangerous. Had I survived these attacks only for the prescribed fix to prove fatal?

I returned to work the next day—and had an attack. Propped up, hoping it was enough to prevent the Magic Pill from giving me a hypertensive stroke, I descended into the darkness alone, no longer having the Mayo Clinic as the light at the end of the tunnel to sustain me. Facing the most difficult kind of test in life, I had dug a hole into my problems one day, only to discover the next day that some jerk had filled it in overnight. But I kept digging, kept pushing forward against the resistance, increasingly hard as it was to do when I kept getting knocked flat. And I stopped taking Mayo's Magic Pill.

Having no explanation to offer, I settled for letting others draw their own conclusions, and spent my most precious resources on my clients. During my attack-free hours, I showed up and looked about the same, except my suits were baggy and my eyes no longer sparkled.

This is what we don't speak of in a profession populated by perfectionists. We don't speak about what lies behind the eyes of beaten-down attorneys. When I was radiant, well, and performing up to my perfectionist standards for bringing my vision to life, I hadn't known what lay behind the defeated looks I saw in other lawyers' eyes. Mine glowed. But then I saw my own eyes grow . . . dim. And I felt hopelessness settle heavily and dampen my spirit. I lost my joy.

I was circling in a shoddy airplane—some days it coasted, other days it hit terrifying turbulence and the hull threatened to break. It became so miserable onboard that I'd have settled for a crash. But I held on for dear life, because the crash freeing me from my defective body would leave my loved ones wrecked.

I'd given my entrepreneurial spirit free rein when envisioning the criminal-defense firm that I had brought to life. And then I had stuffed it in a box and chained it inside, because I was unwilling to face my uncertain health situation. I feared what it meant for my professional life.

My spirit does not respond well to smothering, and fought back. I started to look beyond my new limitations into possibilities. The old me, Ri-ta-lent-less, had the physical ability to realize her vision for her expanding criminal-defense firm. The new Rita couldn't work twelve-hour days, six to seven days a week. Maybe this path had been mine only in passing.

The evolving Rita Spirit showed up as a yearning to write. And I was back to the language I'd used the day I decided to launch my law practice. That day wasn't Someday, it was Now. That day, I was attack-free—no thanks to Mayo's Magic Pill. Whatever I'd do next year or next decade in the ethereal realm of

Someday, on that day I was a business owner, and a criminal-defense lawyer. That day was for the individuals I'd promised to serve. And I was back to that day, with a new twist. Now, I told myself, I will reach within and release my stories. Maybe I'll weave stories like the ones that allowed me to escape when I was trapped inside my body, flattened by an attack. My goal became bringing back a body that could hold her.

I set a new standard for my next healthcare provider. Instead of going to specialists unconcerned for my quality of life because insurance largely covered the medical bills, I'd select the next provider because he or she was dedicated to returning me to wellness. I searched online, and went with my gut.

Twenty minutes into the initial consult, my integrative-medical doctor said, "I think I know exactly what's wrong with you. You have a blood-sugar disorder called reactive hypoglycemia. And you have a dysfunction called adrenal fatigue. I also suspect that you have Lyme disease." He assured me I'd return to good health. I left with an action plan, and peace of mind.

My persistence had paid off. A simple blood test confirmed the identity of what had flattened me: reactive hypoglycemia. We're all subject to sugar spikes and crashes (observe kids after their cotton candy wears off, or adults at work during the afternoon slump). Mine are speedy and severe. When my blood sugar spikes, my insulin charges out to do battle, overzealously destroying even the glucose I need to fuel my body. When my car doesn't have enough fuel to run, it sputters, jerks, and stops on the side of the road; I stammer and lose coordination. My mind becomes murky. Panic strikes as my body shifts into emergency mode. When the arrow hits red, I pass out.

I'd thought my body had turned wimpy on me. In truth, it had endured a blood-sugar disorder, an endocrine dysfunction, and a tick-borne infection. Like the regenerating mutant Wolverine who kept going until ninjas shot him with enough arrows to turn his back into a pincushion, I had trudged along valiantly. I had a new story to tell myself about my body: not wimp—Wolverine. If I followed doctor's orders, I'd regenerate. To regenerate, I had to revamp my life. No Magic Pill existed for reactive hypoglycemia, but changing my lifestyle would allow me to live a healthy life.

Here comes the most painful part of my entrepreneurial path: I had to unchain myself from the captain's wheel to go on medical leave. In the breathing space it created, I allowed my entrepreneurial spirit out of the criminal-defense firm cage. Somewhere along the way, I'd forgotten that my business creation belonged to me. When I withdrew from my active cases and stepped away from my law firm, I thought, sheepishly and in shock, *Who am I, if not a lawyer? If I'm not Rita Johansen of Johansen Law Office?* I had no answer.

Just as I had done in the transitory limbo after law school, before launching my entrepreneurial spirit and focusing it on my criminal-defense firm, I floundered. I had never learned how to BE, period. "I am" had been followed by a descriptor that pointed to how I engaged with the world: a hard worker, an owner, a lawyer. Rest was a foreign concept. I thought if I worked hard enough at it, I would become excellent at this activity.

While trying to rest one day, I observed my beagle, Lexus. I admired the simplicity of her life, the depth of her joy. She didn't have my conditioning. While gazing out at the woods watching for critters to enter the yard, she didn't wonder if that was the most efficient use of her time. Lexus savored the moment. She wagged her tail and shook in anticipation. A squirrel scurried into view. She leapt into action, committed to answering the call to adventure. The critter evaded her, but Lexus bounded about anyway. She went after it and celebrated the thrill of the hunt. Returning to her vantage point, she settled in, tail wagging, content to take it all in again until the next opportunity came her way.

While on medical leave, this realization slipped into my consciousness: *I'm not going back*. I had envisioned a criminal-defense firm that would grow large enough to fill the need I'd discovered for client-centered, emotionally intelligent representation. I now understood that I was unwilling to pay this new, sky-high price to achieve my vision for Johansen Law Office: my health. I allowed my vision to expand to include many practitioners at the helms of many ships. A fleet would have the greatest impact. An armada of radiant practitioners would illuminate this practice area. No longer willing and able to serve at my own helm, I assigned myself a new role: to guide others on how to build seaworthy vessels, and inspire them to set sail.

I committed to my expanded vision and dismantled my own creation. It was an empowering experience. With my wits, willpower, and work ethic, I had built an unconventional criminal-defense practice and claimed my niche in the marketplace. I had used the True to You Approach to grow my law practice, and then later, to launch an independent publishing company to share works such as this one. The principles underlying the True to You Approach are sound and apply to any of your entrepreneurial endeavors, however they evolve.

As you embark on your own bold journey, I caution you against making my biggest mistake: I lost sight of the fact that while my law practice was mine, it didn't define me. You and I are greater than anything we'll create in this shared reality. We're the motive power behind our endeavors.

That's the essence of my message: You're free. Free to explore, to travel down a path and then change direction, to follow the intuition meant to guide you toward your life's purpose. Free to enjoy your life as it passes by each moment.

The True to You Approach is meant to keep you out of a box—be it crafted by others or by your own hand. If your eyes ever dim, remember this majestic word: *FREE*.

ACKNOWLEDGMENTS

Thank you to my husband, Kyle Johansen, who has a steel spine and a big heart, the strength to challenge me, and the compassion to do so with great love; and the other members of my Serenity Circle—Daniel Berg, Jennifer Berg, Dorothy Berg, Paula Meyer, Irina Calciu, Anthony Frascone, and Megan Kelly.

Thanks also to those who have aided my evolution as a businessperson. Most noteworthy is Andy Meyer, who gave me my hands-on experience in growing a small business before I started my solo practice.

Mark Osler, Scott Swanson, Hank Shea, Susan Marsnik, and the many other passionate and proficient educators who fueled my love of learning and built my confidence to rise to meet any intellectual challenge.

The clear-thinking Robert Kahn, who elevated my writing. Any pithy passages are due to his great influence.

Alanna Moravetz, who told me that the legal profession needs people like me. Her words mattered.

Minnesota Women Lawyers, Solo Spectacular, and Women of Words (WOW). I could not have shared my entrepreneurial path with more positive, witty, and encouraging comrades.

To Lynn Cross, editor at Wings for Your Words, who read my beloved brainchild first, gently shaped my words, and affirmed that my work was ready to share.

The serendipitous connections that spurred me to write this book and share it with you now, instead of waiting for the elusive Someday: Peggy Jennings, Roshini Rajkumar, Connie Anderson, Kristen Brown, and Mark LeBlanc.

Profound thanks to the many other generous spirits who have championed me and my entrepreneurial endeavors. My heart overflows at the realization that they are too numerous to name if I want to keep this book short.

HEARTFELT MESSAGE

Thank you, dear Reader, for making time to embark on an entrepreneurial adventure with me! Your feedback, insights, and stories matter to me. I love hearing from readers! I invite you to:

• Review my book on Amazon, Goodreads, or another reader-community website;

• Email me at Rita@RitaJohansen.com;

• Visit my website, www.RitaJohansen.com, to discover more about me and my work to empower entrepreneurs;

• Check out and follow my blog, *True to You: A Revolutionary Way to Transform Your Life*;

• Like my Facebook page and post your comments;

• Tweet me, @TrueRita, #TruetoYouBook; and

• Connect with me on LinkedIn.

Please make requests to use this copyrighted material elsewhere (e.g., training materials, courses, blog posts, articles, books, workshops) by email to Johansen@Johansen-Justice.com, or mail to Johansen Justice, P.O. Box 14, Anoka, MN 55303.

I leave you with this gentle reminder: Someday is today! Go!

With great appreciation,

Rita Johansen

35487594R00084

Made in the USA
Charleston, SC
10 November 2014